THE EUROPEAN MONEY
PUZZLE

THE EUROPEAN MONEY PUZZLE

Peter Readman with Jonathan Davies
Michael Hoare David Poole

Michael Joseph · London

First published in Great Britain by
Michael Joseph Ltd
52 Bedford Square
London WC1B 3EF
1973

ISBN 0 7181 1131 1 (hardbound)
ISBN 0 7181 1132 X (paperback)

Set and printed in Great Britain by
Western Printing Services, Ltd, Bristol,
in Imprint type, ten point two-point leaded, and bound by
Dorstel Press, Harlow

Contents

5

Preface

The authors, who are employed by different City Institutions, but who work together under the name 'GEM', first met at INSEAD, the European Business School at Fontainebleau. While there they carried out a survey on developments in European banking which formed the basis of the first 'GEM' Report.

After INSEAD the authors returned to their individual jobs in the City, but encouraged by the success of their report went on to give talks and contribute articles to financial papers and journals. However, realising that banking was only part of the picture, and dissatisfied with their understanding about European finance, GEM decided to undertake a more ambitious project. This was to find out how the financial markets of the Continent work and to attempt to judge how European financial systems would develop in an enlarged Community. To this end members of GEM interviewed over 200 bankers, financiers and members of the European Commission as well as carrying out the more usual methods of research in turgid Central Bank reports and worthy academic tomes.

The result, the authors hope, is a practical analysis of Continental financial markets with some pointers to their likely future development and how these will be affected by Community policies. The book also attempts to point to the financial opportunities and difficulties facing Britain in a United Europe. It is impossible to treat such a wide subject in so few pages, and the authors have considered those areas of European finance which interest them most. This explains the book's concentration on financial institutions and the longer-term markets at the expense of shipping, insurance and commodity markets which also form a vital part of the City's activities.

The authors are not academics and have tried to view all issues especially in the political sphere as dispassionately as possible. They do believe, however, that despite the vicissitudes of day-to-day political life,

Europe must eventually unite and this book is based on that premise.

To understand the subject some figures are unfortunately necessary, but these have been kept to a minimum, and are presented in the form of tables. While statistics have been culled from the most respectable sources, it is well to remember that within individual countries figures are often unreliable, while between countries bases of comparison are rarely the same.

The authors would like to thank all those who generously gave up so much of their valuable time, without whom this book could not have been written. They are unfortunately too numerous to mention, but the authors hope that those who have the patience to read further, will recognise their contributions. Special thanks must, however, be extended to Mr John Weiner, a member of the London Stock Exchange, who went to considerable trouble to introduce us to some of his many friends in Europe, to Lee Remmers of INSEAD and to Ann Gosman whose patience in typing the many drafts of this book was remarkable. We would also like most particularly to thank our employers, especially Charter Consolidated and the Ionian Bank, for their support and encouragement. We are most grateful to Tony Hambro for allowing us to reproduce his invaluable paper on the London markets as an appendix.

Last but not least the authors wish to make it clear that the views expressed in this book are purely personal and they regret the book's many shortcomings and omissions.

Introduction

One of Britain's greatest contributions to an enlarged Europe may well prove to be the services and skills of the City of London.

The 1970 White Paper on 'Britain and the European Communities' assumed that 'the City of London should bring benefits not only to the United Kingdom but to other members of the EEC as well. The City can offer a wide range of financial and commercial services which is unrivalled outside the United States. With greater awareness of these facilities, both we and our future partners can expect to gain increasing advantage.' This reflected a general feeling, still prevalent, that British financial practices would not only be easily adapted to but should also be welcome on the Continent where financial markets were considered not merely badly organised but undeveloped with much to gain from City expertise.

In spite of the post-war decline of sterling, no one can contest that the City has maintained its position as the leading financial market in Europe. In comparison the financial markets of the other member countries are far less important. The City now contributes £600 million per annum to the British Balance of Payments but, for historical reasons, it has concentrated its activities primarily on the Commonwealth and the United States and direct business in Europe has been negligible. Indeed the City has recently been running a £70 million deficit on invisible transactions with Community countries, and although this can be partly explained by the incidence of interest on Eurodollar loans, the Community remains largely uncharted waters.

Despite the hazards of an unexplored environment, Britain's membership of the European Community offers considerable opportunities. However, few markets can be successfully exploited without a comprehensive knowledge of potential customers' requirements and the extent to which these may be profitably satisfied and while the City's services may be more sophisticated it would be making an error of judgement if it failed to realise that the British way of doing things is not necessarily applicable to a Continental environment. Continental attitudes to finance are very different from the British and it is not surprising therefore that the financial systems that have evolved on the Continent bear little resemblance to the intricate network of specialised financial institutions of which the City is justly so proud. Indeed it seems reasonable to suggest that it is the very lack of comparable Continental institutions and markets which makes it so difficult for the City to operate effectively on the Continent. To make matters worse Community legislation will encourage an increasingly unified European financial system which is bound to take on some of the characteristics of Continental financial markets least advantageous to London. Thus success for the City will not merely depend on the resources which are diverted to investigating these new markets and on its ability to adapt to unfamiliar methods, traditions and rules but also on how well it puts its case when Community legislation is framed.

Chapter One

The Economic Community—
Myth and Reality

The European Economic Community has now been in existence for fifteen years and before examining what it has achieved during this time it is worth briefly stating what has led to Britain's decision to join and therefore indirectly why this book has been written.

During the late 1940s and 1950s Britain as the victor looked on dispassionately as the defeated states of Europe attempted to close ranks in order to rebuild their shattered nations and defuse the dreaded Germany once and for all. At this time Britain saw little reason to associate herself too closely with these developments as she envisaged a much greater future for herself as an important world power at the focal point of the three main capitalist blocks—the Commonwealth, the United States of America and Europe.

However, the wisdom of this strategy was gradually called into question by the political, economic and social forces of the post-war years. The Suez Crisis, a major political rebuff, revealed that Britain was virtually powerless to act against an impertinent pirate. The failure of Blue Streak demonstrated that an independent nuclear deterrent was no longer feasible. The campaigns for nuclear disarmament and the antics of the 'Angry Young Men' revealed the pangs of self-doubt gripping the nation. The frequent sterling crises publicly demonstrated Britain's economic plight at a time when European growth rates had risen well out of Britain's league. All in all it was a painful period during which the country came to realise that she was no longer a major world power and that her economic future was in jeopardy.

Some new strategy had to be devised. There were various alternatives. One possibility was to strengthen ties with the Commonwealth, but the major Commonwealth countries were going their own political and economic ways and the irreversible trend was a loosening of ties between the member states. There was the alternative of developing the special relationship with the United States and creating some sort of North Atlantic Free Trade association; such ideas met with little enthusiasm across the Atlantic and in any case would have eventually led to Britain being swallowed up by the United States—a most unpalatable prospect to many Englishmen. The hastily formed EFTA worked reasonably well as a customs union, but offered little further opportunity of development for Britain, the most dominant member. There were thus only two real alternatives left; either Britain adopted a negative attitude and remained a fading star in an increasingly dazzling firmament or she took the positive step of trying to play a major role in a truly European Community.

What then is Britain joining? It is joining an elite club of the richer Western European nations which have decided to work more closely together for peace and prosperity after the disastrous experiences of the first half of this century. The club's foundations are in the European Coal and Steel Community which was established in 1951, but it did not itself take shape until 1957 when the Treaty of Rome set the seal on the Six's overt aims to work together towards economic union. Since then the European Community has been dominated by the two most powerful members, France and Germany. Indeed it has even been suggested that it was only ever formed as a result of an agreement between France and Germany that in return for the French lending the Germans political respectability, the Germans would agree to a penal tax on imported foodstuffs which would directly support French farmers. It is not surprising therefore that the main tangible achievements of the Community have been the establishment of a Common Agricultural policy, which by fixing high minimum prices for Community produced foodstuffs protects its many inefficient small farmers, and an agreement to reduce customs barriers between member countries. Trade between Community countries has risen more sharply than external trade and it has been suggested that economic growth in some member countries, notably Belgium, has been given a direct stimulus by the formation of the Community. There have also been some moves towards standardisation in such fields as taxation. But in terms of practical achievement this adds up to very little when compared with the failure of more fundamental co-operation on technological, industrial and economic planes which sadly have not measured up to the expectations of the Community's founders.

Without commenting on the historical arguments about joining the Community, or on Britain's failure to play a formative role when the Community was still at its embryonic stage, it is clear that Britain is now all but committed to a path that will eventually lead to some kind of United Europe. Despite the lack of real progress so far Britain is playing for higher stakes than a right to contribute to the European butter mountain, and to enjoy reductions on external tariffs which could in the short-term hurt British industries. The seeds of economic union have now been sown, and as with the Zollverein in nineteenth-century Germany, political unification seems merely a matter of time, even if a man of the stature of Bismarck is needed to overcome the mistrust and destructive national self-interest which have been the salient characteristics of the Community to date.

At the moment it is difficult to see how nine proud and independent nations are to be persuaded to work together for their mutual benefit. The Treaty of Rome looks towards the free movement of capital, goods and labour but it is not clear as to how this is to be achieved. The current arguments raging on whether economic, monetary or political union should be sought first not only conceal the major long-term problem facing the Community, that of producing viable regional policies, but fail to appreciate how the Community is in fact developing. For this we must turn to the European Commission soldiering on relentlessly in Brussels.

The Commission is the Community's Civil Service—the supranational power behind the national thrones represented in the Council of Ministers. The Treaty of Rome requires the Commission to act completely independently and to ensure that the best interests of the Community are observed at all times; indeed despite the fact that many of its members are drawn from the national civil services they are not supposed to be subject to the influence of their respective governments.

The Commission is, however, something more than a civil service for it has powers not merely to implement but also to initiate Community legislation. As part of its role in initiating new policies, the Commission has a free hand to tackle any matter falling within the Treaty of Rome, and the Treaty is so notoriously vague in a number of key areas that the numerous lawyers on the Commission have had little difficulty in ensuring that its activities are virtually unrestricted. A cynical English observer in Brussels commented, 'They consume more paper and produce more half-baked ideas and recommendations than all the governments of the Six put together.' However, it would be naïve to assume that the Commission is a toothless bulldog merely because few of these recommendations have so far been considered, let alone implemented.

In almost any action the Community decides to take, it must turn to the Commission for ideas and advice. Thus the Commission, in building up its own information and prejudices about Europe in the context of the Six, has been laying the foundation for legislation that could be implemented sooner than many people imagine. The thin end of the wedge has already been seen in the anti-trust measures taken under Articles 85 and 86 against Continental Can and more recently ICI and in a wide variety of minor legislation such as that affecting the size of lorries to be allowed on British roads. Looming ominously on the horizon are a number of directives designed to harmonise various aspects of company law such as the recent proposal for worker participation on company boards, which, if implemented, will have far-reaching consequences for British industry and indeed the City.

The reason that so little of the Commission's labour has borne fruit to date is that the decision-making power resides in the Council of Ministers made up of representatives of each of the national governments. Up to now there has been no sign of the national governments in any way lessening their control of the Commission or attempting to establish any other supranational decision-making authority. Thus the pessimist could conclude that there is unlikely to be any more significant progress in the next fifteen years than there has been in the past, for few people would suggest that it is possible to reach the degree of co-ordination necessary for complicated economic or monetary policies when vital decision-making power is situated in nine separate places.

The optimist can take heart in the opinion of a senior French representative of the Commission who did not hide for a moment that deadlock had been reached on the fundamental problem of the co-ordination of economic policy. He did however say that the Commission is 'chipping away at the minor problems, attempting to create a base of common interest, from which to tackle the greater problems'. In this way people throughout the Community in a variety of positions and occupations are forced to work together to try to find solutions to trivial matters. This will in turn induce them to subdue little by little their nationalist prejudices and interests for the good of the Community as a whole. Until a sufficient degree of mutual trust is established throughout the Community, national governments, which are of course dependent on the votes of the people they represent, will be unable to surrender that part of their sovereignty and autonomy which is essential for the co-ordination of any form of economic policy.

Undoubtedly to European idealists, romantics and Commissioners progress will seem slow, but it is well to recall the picture of Europe twenty-five years ago. The scars of the past few centuries cannot be healed overnight and to the historian developments since the war have been considerable. Of course the dreams of the Fathers of Europe are no longer realistic just as the ideas of the seventies and eighties will probably bear little relation to what sort of Community will exist in 1990, but in the words of King Lear, 'Nothing will come of nothing', and at least a start has been made.

It is, however, to be hoped that the Community will not follow King Lear into the madhouse. There have been signs that in an attempt to achieve the smallest degree of progress Community members have had to resort to compromises whose results have often been the erection of barriers as formidable as any already existing between the member states. Some convinced Europeans have even suggested that it is the deliberate policy of the Commission to push plans containing unworkable elements which are bound to lead to crises, as this is the surest way of gathering national decision-makers together in an urgent effort to find solutions. Nowhere is there a better example of this possibly unconscious process at work than in the controversial fields of economic and monetary union.

The questions of economic and monetary union, both fundamental to the establishment of a genuine Economic Community, first arose in February 1969. Raymond Barre, now Vice-President of the Commission, raised the subject in a paper in which he argued that as a result of the successful abolition of tariff barriers and the workings of the Common Agricultural Policy, the trade and economies of the Six were far more dependent on each other than before the EEC existed. Consequently the economy of one member country could be substantially influenced by events in another and to remedy this, he suggested joint economic planning and mutually consistent economic policies to avoid the contagious effect on the whole Community of imbalance in any one member. Barre emphasised the need for economic policies, but in complete contrast, Pierre Werner, in presenting a plan for economic and monetary union in May 1970, suggested that the first step should be the implementation of monetary union.

During the discussions which followed, a clear split developed between the 'monetarists' and the 'economists', and more fundamentally between those who favoured intergovernmental co-operation and those who favoured federalism as the best means of furthering the Community's ends. France, the main protagonist of the monetarist cause, saw fixed exchange rates as the safest way of safeguarding the Common Agricultural Policy, dependent as it is on common prices which have to be readjusted when exchange rates change. She also saw a Common European currency as the surest way of reducing Europe's dependence on the dollar. At the same time there could have been serious disadvantages in having too great a degree of economic co-operation, as this would have allowed Germany a say in France's economic management. The Germans on the other hand have always supported the economist and federalist cause, as they are particularly afraid of imported inflation and also feel they should not be forced to finance possible French deficits without any effective means of influencing the economic policies which lead to the deficits. They therefore took the view that the co-ordination of the separate economies was essential before fixed exchange rates could be adopted. This however implied a far greater degree of political integration than was acceptable to the French who have always shown the greatest reluctance to surrender any part of their national economic management to supranational Community institutions.

Despite these differences a modified Werner plan enabled both sides to reach in 1971 a compromise whereby union was to proceed on both fronts—economic and monetary—concurrently, although at first sight it appeared that it still took no account of regional or other fundamental economic problems. As a result of this compromise the Germans finally gave in to the French, but they insisted on a prudence clause which allowed them to withdraw between the third and fifth year if they were not satisfied with the extent to which the other member states had co-ordinated their economic policies under central Community control.

They never had the embarrassment of implementing the clause, as world events overtook the Community's agreement. The German and Dutch floating in May was followed by the dollar crisis in August and finally by the Smithsonian agreement in December. The events of 1971 were therefore a clear indication that economic pressures even outside the Community could upset the plan for monetary union and many people thought this was an excellent opportunity for the Commission to reconsider their ideas. However in the prevailing calm after the Smithsonian agreement, the Community elected to continue on Werner's path of narrowing the margins between the existing currencies, thus guaranteeing future monetary chaos and giving foreign exchange dealers ample time to prepare for the next crisis.

The Werner plan is based on the concept of gradually narrowing the exchange rates between the Community currencies until they can be irrevocably interlocked.* Even as modified in 1972 the plan was bound

---

* The ultimate aim of the Werner plan is to have a single currency circulating throughout the Community managed by a Community Central Bank. The means by which this is to be achieved is that members of the Community agree to intervene in each other's currencies in order to keep all Community currencies within a fixed range of each other. This range, initially set at 2·25 per cent, will be narrowed until the individual national currencies have been locked together so that no fluctuations are possible and full convertibility exists. Exchange control between Community members will be dismantled with the result that the domestic financial markets of the member states will be merged into a single

to put intolerable strains on the economies of certain member countries for it is not possible to merge the currencies of countries with widely differing rates of inflation and growth without in some way compensating for these differences with supporting economic policies. The Community, however, had not found it possible to reach agreement on the supporting economic policies. Since there were various other alternatives open to the Community it would appear that the Commission expressly decided to opt for this particular course in the knowledge that it was bound to lead to crises and thus publicly demonstrate the need for parallel economic policies. Crises have occurred, the first one before the ink on the agreement was dry, but each time high-level national decision-makers have been forced to meet to resolve the problem and in the process must have become more aware of the missing economic ingredients. It therefore seems as if the Commission's policy of pushing plans containing unworkable or missing elements is paying off for almost every time there has been a crisis, progress has been made.

A good example of this increased co-operation was the recent sterling crisis when the central banks and national governments did work very closely together to support the pound under the arrangements of March 1972 whereby the members of the Community agreed to intervene in each other's currencies in order to keep all Community currencies within the 2·25 per cent band. Highlighted by this crisis was the pitifully small sum set aside to defend the narrowed band of exchange rates. The total of $4 billion of short- and medium-term credits originally established to aid countries with balance of payments problems was seen to be hopelessly inadequate to cope with speculative flows harnessed to a Eurodollar market of $65 billion.

It seems therefore as if the Commission's policy of recommending the Werner plan, despite its unworkable elements, has achieved a certain degree of success. But it will be a long time before these policies are in fact implemented and meanwhile monetary union will be unable to progress much further without leading to regular currency crises.

It is worth examining briefly the two main alternatives which faced the Community: of placing greater emphasis on economic or on monetary union. While the goal of economic co-operation may appear perfectly feasible on paper, it is difficult to see how member countries, notoriously open to pressures of self-interest, can be forced to adopt the necessary internal fiscal and monetary policies at a day-to-day operating level. The Commission's problem has therefore been to create the pressure on member countries so that they see the necessity for

Community domestic market containing some form of common exchange control vis-à-vis non-community countries.

co-ordinated economic policies and it has tried to achieve this by putting the monetary cart before the economic horse. The recent establishment of a high-level economic co-ordination committee is an encouraging sign that the economists' pleas are no longer falling on deaf ears but considerably greater progress in the economic field is required before it will be possible to see whether monetary union throughout the Community is a sensible goal or not.

Despite the fact that at this stage monetary union is unworkable it is at least easier to monitor and has met with less initial resistance from the countries involved. There are various ways in which the Commission could have aimed at monetary union. The simplest would merely have been to wait until one currency emerged as being generally acceptable in the other member countries, as for example the US dollar is acceptable in Panama. A more positive course would be to create an artificial parallel currency such as an EMU or Europa,* which would be similar to a Eurodollar, except that parity changes with the dollar and more control over the currency would be possible. Such a scheme would enable the advantages of monetary integration to be seen and experienced almost immediately without impairing the capacity of member countries to deal with their balance of payments difficulties by altering their parities. Its proponents believe it avoids the dangers inherent in a premature locking of currencies, which, by eliminating devaluation as a method of correcting balance of payments deficits, are such that they could lead to the disintegration of the Community. They also believe that such a scheme would achieve capital market harmonisation sooner than would otherwise be the case. However, the danger of changing to a plan which does not affect the individual currencies them-

* The Federal Trust recently published a report in which it outlined its plan for the Europa. The new European currency unit would circulate throughout the Community in parallel with existing national currencies. In return for an agreed proportion of national central bank reserves and a quota of national currency, the Community central bank would distribute an equivalent amount of Europas to the national central banks. These Europas would be used for a variety of purposes including eventually private circulation and a short time after their introduction would replace the dollar as the intervention currency in European foreign exchange markets. The national central banks would maintain a narrow band of fluctuation between their currencies and the Europa while the Community bank would maintain a wide band between the Europa and the dollar. When the Community had reached the measure of economic co-ordination enabling monetary integration to be implemented the national currencies of the Community would be withdrawn and replaced by the Europa.

This sort of scheme has a distinct advantage over the alternative of adopting one of the existing European currencies as the international currency in that the country whose currency was selected would obviously wish to determine its monetary policy with a view to domestic rather than European conditions. Similar considerations have always applied to the Eurodollar market.

selves is that the pressures for co-ordinated economic policies which have arisen as a direct result of the Werner plan for monetary union will largely disappear. There is therefore a risk that the psychological progress which has so far been achieved will vanish into thin air.

In all these discussions, regional policy, not only one of the keys to monetary union but fundamental to the long-term success of the Community, has been conveniently forgotten. Monetary union throughout Europe will mean that any long-term regional imbalance in growth, wage or inflation rates will cause chronic economic problems for the poorer members unless these imbalances can be offset by regional subsidies. With the present background of national self-interest, it seems inevitable that such subsidies could only be implemented on a sufficiently large scale by a powerful central authority able to overrule the parochial claims of richer members, who would have to provide the necessary finance. The fact that regional policies have been almost totally ignored during the past decade is scarcely surprising given the domination of the Community of Six by France and Germany, neither of which suffers from drastic regional problems. France however has made very sure that its declining agricultural areas have been nursed by the Community budget. It would seem logical that countries with declining industrial areas should receive similar Community benefits, although this argument does not appeal to our agronome friends.

The problems of managing these policies and in effect splitting the cake between nine very greedy children are only just beginning to emerge and even at a national level successful regional policies have proved difficult to implement, as Britain's experience in Scotland and Northern Ireland shows. The fact that in an enlarged Community the difficulties will be considerably greater has important implications for Britain which not only suffers disproportionately low investment and high inflation rates but is also at an immutable geographical disadvantage. By subscribing to the present plans for monetary union she will eventually find herself deprived of devaluation, her chief weapon against her exports becoming prohibitively uncompetitive in international and particularly Continental markets. Britain will therefore be extremely foolish to support a plan which will turn it into the Scotland of the Community unless it can ensure that it is compensated for the loss of the power to devalue by means of effective regional and industrial policies. These in turn can only be implemented by a politically united Europe and even then success is not assured as is readily demonstrated by the failure of United Kingdom regional policies, recognised as the most advanced in Europe.

Britain's entry into the Community could therefore be a decisive factor in achieving a significantly greater emphasis on co-ordinated economic policies. But as far as Britain is concerned half-measures will not suffice; having taken the decision to join Europe she must, if only for reasons of simple economic self-interest, abandon the pretence of self-sufficiency, withdraw from the anti-supranational camp and join the Germans and Dutch in all-out advocacy of European political union.

Chapter Two

The Whys and Whims of
Capital Markets

Before considering individual countries in detail it is worth examining
in outline the underlying structure and economic importance of the
wide range of different markets which make up a country's 'financial
market'. Despite the many different functions fulfilled by such markets
they have one all-important economic function, that of attracting personal savings, transforming them from short- to long-term if necessary,
and finally channelling them cheaply and effectively into investment.
Not all savings move through such markets. Of the three broad categories of savers in Western economic systems—the state, enterprises
and households—it is household savings which are the principal source
of new money for financial markets. The state's savings are usually
channelled directly to government and local authority projects such as
building schools, hospitals and motorways. Business savings in the form
of cash flow are normally reinvested to finance expansion and modernisation of equipment. Household savings are therefore the only large
source of uncommitted funds.

Financial markets can be looked at from two points of view; that of
the private individual wishing to safeguard his savings, and that of a
business or government wishing to spend them. The placing of savings
in the various financial markets is not the only option open to the
household saver as his choice also ranges through buying tangibles
such as property, gold or antiques. Financially, he can hold cash,
lend his money for a fixed return, or place his funds at greater risk
by buying shares in a company. On the other hand, the businessman
wishing to raise money to invest faces only two main choices: obtaining
funds at a fixed or floating rate of interest, or selling a share of his
business.

It is obvious therefore that the requirements of the saver and of the
businessman are usually very different and it is the object of the various

financial markets to match the needs of both in the most efficient way. Savers on the whole like to feel they can withdraw their savings if they need them and so tend to commit them to short-term investments. Businessmen on the other hand need long-term funds. One of the major roles of financial intermediaries is therefore that of transformation or conversion of short-term savings into longer-term funds suitable for investment; a good example of this process at work is that of the building societies in Britain which accept comparatively short-term deposits but yet lend for up to, say, twenty-five years. On the Continent the scale of this transformation process is much greater than in Britain as a far higher proportion of household savings are short-term and Continental institutions which attract long-term savings, often in contractual form, are less well developed than in Britain. Continental governments have historically intervened to aid the banks in the dangerous process of transformation which has been the cause of most bank failures—that is, breaking the golden maxim of borrowing short and lending long. Increasing facilities for refinancing loans at central banks and other government institutions make the process considerably safer and recently medium-term lending, especially in the Eurodollar markets, has benefited through the invention of the roll-over loan, whereby interest rates are not fixed but tied to local short-term borrowing costs.

The term capital market is used to refer to the market for long-term finance and it is to this that business must turn to raise its capital in the form of shares and bonds. The generally accepted mixture of the two, or level of gearing, in a company's capital structure is not fixed but set by local financial custom. Gearing levels vary enormously between countries and are for example much higher in Germany than in Britain, although different national methods of asset valuation make comparisons difficult. Gearing also varies according to the type of industry; a high-risk industry is likely to have more equity finance than bond or debt finance so that it can be certain of servicing the interest payable on the debt even in bad years.

On a different plane the equity and bond markets also fulfil an important secondary function when, for example, a saver buys or sells shares which are already in circulation. This action will only result in an exchange of ownership and no money will be received by the company. If, on the other hand, the saver buys a premium bond or subscribes to a rights issue his savings pass directly into the hands of the government or businessmen rather than back in the pockets of other savers. The distinction between the primary issues function and the secondary trading function of capital markets is often blurred but it is extremely important, as, economically, secondary markets are only of benefit if they improve the process of transformation and facilitate the workings of primary markets, for active dealing is of no value in itself. Thus developed secondary markets can have the advantage of encouraging a greater flow of savings into long-term investment enabling companies to raise finance more cheaply. On the Continent there is a lack of good secondary markets which in turn has a detrimental effect on primary markets, although this is not such a serious disadvantage as many have suggested, owing to the intervention of public institutions. Stock market devotees would do well to remember that active betting does not make the horses run faster.

The main function of a capital market is therefore to provide long-term finance for industry. This is of particular importance in Europe where the past two decades have seen accelerating wage rates, which in most countries have increased personal savings faster than company profits. This is a trend which shows no sign of slowing down and if European companies are to maintain the high levels of investment of the past decade they will have to rely increasingly on external finance provided by the financial markets. Also if Europe is ever to compete effectively with the United States and Japan, industrial investment must take place at much the same sort of rate. Capital supplied to American manufacturing corporations has recently been rising about twice as fast as output, and although statistics for Europe are difficult to compute, capital formation has certainly not been so rapid. Whereas American capital supply runs at about 30 per cent of value added, in Europe this figure is only about 20–25 per cent. Since the rate of cash flow is also relatively lower in Europe than in the United States the need for new capital in Europe is enormous.

The creators of the European Community clearly foresaw the increasing future needs for capital and assumed that as their various plans for economic integration proceeded pressures would build up on the capital markets to provide finance on an increasingly European as opposed to domestic scale. Although they did not specifically provide for the development of a unified European capital market in the Treaty of Rome, Article 67 instructed member states gradually to remove restrictions and abolish discriminatory treatment affecting capital movements between them, so far as may be necessary to ensure the proper workings of the Common Market. This is a somewhat vague clause but under the Treaty, the Common Market will only be finally achieved when there is free circulation of people, goods and capital.

The Commission set about giving effect to Article 67 in two directives issued in May 1960 and December 1962. These distinguished between capital movements to be unconditionally freed, and those to be conditionally freed, and instructed member countries to abolish unconditionally all restrictions on direct and portfolio investment, investment in real estate, certain personal transactions and short- and medium-termed credit linked to commercial transactions. The conditionally freed capital movements included the issue of a national company's shares on a foreign stock exchange, the issue of a foreign company's shares on a national stock exchange and certain other share transactions. The conditional element allowed countries to retain control over these matters if they thought them essential for their national economic goals. A measure of the extent to which member countries were prepared to co-operate is perhaps indicated by the fact that France, Italy and Holland accepted the conditional clause gratefully and took no action until a further directive was issued in February 1967 instructing these countries to relax their controls.

These directives did bring about greater financial flows in the Community, but were never intended by themselves to create an integrated European capital market. However, as a result of greater economic integration in other areas, the Commission decided in 1966 that the time had come to consider this subject more closely and commissioned Professor Segré and a group of experts to study the problems confronting the domestic capital markets of the Community. The ensuing Segré report was based on the premise that the financial needs of increasingly integrated European industry would necessitate much greater co-operation between the capital markets than there was in 1966. This would in turn mean bringing financial institutions and mechanisms in individual member countries more into line with one another. European industry would thus have easier access to greater volumes of more varied forms of European capital while savers could choose from a much wider range of investment possibilities.

However, the report in no way minimised the difficulties of this process of integration and it is without doubt the most thorough analysis yet of the differences between the individual capital markets of the Community. Many of its findings and recommendations are as valid today as they were in 1966, for little practical progress has since been made. The enormous differences between national capital markets means that integration is still out of the question, for the simple reason that some countries have considerably more to lose than others. In this instance France would have to give ground and although Gallic charm sometimes persuades others to forgo their interests Gallic logic requires that France should never be the loser. Segré's practical recommendations were therefore primarily directed to eliminating differences in the individual capital markets so that eventual integration would be made easier.

Although certain national governments have reformed and are reforming aspects of their individual markets, the main reason for lack of progress at Community level is that European demands for capital have simply not materialised to the extent which was envisaged in 1966. Despite much talk of the internationalisation of European industry, there have only been few cross-national mergers and even these have only been partially successful. National governments protecting their own self-interests have blocked several attempts at cross-frontier take-overs such as the British Rollmakers bid for Marichal-Ketin and Equity and Law Life's bid for Union des Propriétaires Belges. Apart from government intervention most businessmen have been discouraged by the very considerable obstacles that still exist to cross-frontier mergers, ranging from cultural differences to the often irreconcilable legal, fiscal and accountancy regulations. Attempts have been made by the Community to reduce some of the practical problems by, for example, harmonising certain taxation and legal regulations and making moves towards the incorporation of a purely European Company possible. There is however now a current of caution running through the Commission and reduced enthusiasm in general for cross-frontier mergers. Indeed industrial integration across borders, with its ensuing demand for pan-European finance, is certainly not on the scale that many once predicted.

Joint technological development has been little more encouraging and in any case has rarely demanded finance on a cross-frontier scale. A major reason for this is the link between advanced technology and defence. States are reluctant to be dependent on others for their defence requirements, and much technological innovation relies on Research and Development sponsored by national governments for defence purposes. Public sector orders are vital for firms operating in the field of aeronautics, electronics, computers and nuclear power and no firm can afford to sever links with its own government in the absence of a European alternative. Few attempts therefore at international technological co-operation have been successful, an exception being the aircraft industry where there are several joint development projects. Technological development in Europe has thus continued to take place on a national basis as indeed has the rationalisation of industry. One of the most glaring examples has been the motor-car industry where the last five years has seen the formation of the British Leyland Motor Corporation, the takeovers of NSU by Volkswagen and Lancia by Fiat and the joint engine project of Peugeot and Renault.

This picture of European industry and technology contrasts very sharply with American companies in Europe. With a few notable exceptions such as Unilever and Shell, the only truly European firms are subsidiaries of American multi-nationals. It seems, sadly, as if it is the Americans rather than the Europeans who realise the potential for manufacturing and trading on a European scale. These multi-national companies do demand capital on an international scale but their needs have been met not by domestic European capital but by American capital in Europe via the Eurodollar market. Some large European companies and even governments have also found it cheaper to meet their financing needs in this market.

The existence of the Eurodollar market as the only truly international market in Europe has relieved the pressure on European domestic capital markets, which have remained to varying degrees controlled and restricted by national governments. It is not surprising therefore that the national financial markets of the different European countries have remained independent. Differences of history, tradition, national temperament and industrial and political development have ensured that each particular financial market has its own special characteristics, and even today different social priorities and educational systems lead to divergent trends. But before considering the workings of the individual markets in more detail, it is worth investigating the two areas in which developments have taken place at anything other than a purely national level. The first of these is the Eurodollar market and the second, certain trends in European banking. It must be depressing for the proponents of a United Europe that in neither case have the institutions of the Community played a significant role.

Chapter Three

Eurodollars and Eurobanking

The Eurodollar and Eurobond Markets

The growth of the Eurodollar* market is undoubtedly the most important single financial development in Europe since the war.

While to the economist the workings of the market present all sorts of problems, to the industrialist or banker a Eurodollar is something relatively simple. For the industrialist a Eurodollar is merely a loan denominated in dollars which he can obtain from his bank, convert into local currency and use, either for a funding operation or for an investment project. Knowing the relevant rates, and bearing in mind the exchange risk, he can compare fairly simply the comparative costs of a Eurodollar and an ordinary bank loan. Likewise from the bankers' point of view Eurodollars are merely another currency in which he can operate in much the same way as he does in his local currency—he borrows from one set of customers and lends to another most of what he has received, but at a higher rate of interest. The source of Eurodollars is also simple. When a banker outside the US receives a foreign credit, say a dollar, from a customer, he would normally convert it at once into his own currency so as to be able to make profitable use of the proceeds. If instead of converting he retains the dollar, or lends it on, he has effectively if unwittingly created a Eurodollar.

It is thus apparent that a Eurodollar is no less than a money in its own right. While clearly related to the dollar in some ways, the Eurodollar must be regarded as an entirely separate currency, albeit with no apparent domicile, central bank or mint. The Eurodollar market is a further money market, parallel and related to the traditional national markets, but with its own separate interest rate structure, institutions

* There are other Eurocurrencies, e.g. Euromarks, in which markets have grown up alongside the far more important Eurodollar market; it is therefore simpler to discuss in Eurodollar terms, but most points can be extended fairly easily to other currencies.

and unwritten rules. There is of course nothing new in the concept of such a market, for example, the Indian government's pre-war use of sterling, but never before has a market developed on such a vast scale.

Certain fundamental factors have influenced the growth of the Eurodollar market, to wit, the supply and demand for funds, the relative efficiency of the market and the need for operations to be both legally possible and institutionally viable. The Russians are sometimes credited with creating the original Eurodollar market when in the late fifties they lent their excess dollars to various European banks, preferring relatively unfavourable interest rates to trusting their precious hard currency to the Americans. A further stimulus to the supply of funds was Regulation 'Q', whereby US banks were restricted in the maximum rates payable on dollar deposits in the United States. This was a considerable incentive to companies to keep dollar funds outside the US rather than to repatriate them.

Recently supply has tended to become a limiting rather than stimulating factor since in the long-term it is linked to the US deficit, and in the short-term to the part central banks play in the deliberate purchase or sale of dollars. This latter is not the control it might appear, because of the side effects on local currencies of which perhaps the Deutschmark is the best-known example.

On the demand side the main incentives to the increased borrowings of Eurodollars have arisen through controls imposed on alternative sources of finance. In Britain the sterling crisis of 1957 resulted in that currency not only becoming excessively expensive (bank rate 7 per cent), but restrictions being imposed on the use of sterling bills to finance trade between non-residents. As a result the accepting houses were forced to find an alternative currency and the Eurodollar market was born. In America the deficits of the late sixties with the resultant restrictions on the export of investment dollars forced US subsidiaries abroad to find an alternative source of funds. The US deficit inspired a further stimulus in the profitable relending of vast amounts of Eurodollars back to the States to benefit from the shortage of dollars under the impact of monetary restraint. Another demand for Eurodollars comes from currency hedging. A desire to profit or at least not to lose from an anticipated change in a country's exchange parity can stimulate the growth of the Eurodollar market. While in volume terms this does not contribute greatly to the size of the market, the suddenness of such operations can have a marked effect on interest rates.

Eurobanking avoids several major restrictions and safeguards found in ordinary national banking. The resulting efficiency, or competitive advantage has been a considerable incentive to the growth of the market. The national restrictions include reserve requirements for the safety of the banking system; money supply and credit controls imposed in the interests of the national economy; restrictions on the free movement of interest rates, and the various cartels operated by national banks. Thus, while from the borrowers' point of view the market has the advantage of being anonymous, flexible, uncontrolled, and generally cheaper, there are naturally commensurate disadvantages, of which perhaps the most important is the lack of a lender of last resort to support the market in a crisis. Thus one of the major weaknesses of the Eurodollar market is that the default of a final borrower, if sufficiently large, could in theory, by means of a chain effect or negative multiplier, disrupt the entire system. Certain economists see a potential danger in the large sums occasionally lent to the Communists who have, however, so far behaved in an exemplary fashion.

For such a market to grow up the main institutional requirements are naturally an adequate infrastructure of relevant expertise and banking contacts. In this the United Kingdom has been the best endowed amongst European countries. However, in view of the improvement in world communications, there are many countries which by importing some expertise could set up a market with costs, such as rents, well below those of London. Legal restrictions may differ between countries, but the principal one in the past has been of exchange control or other controls on foreign currency operations. It should be noted that the Bank of England has been sufficiently farsighted to avoid excessive restrictions on transactions not involving sterling and this not only permitted a faster growth of the Eurodollar market, but also encouraged its being centred on London.

There has been considerable academic debate over the size or even existence of the Eurodollar multiplier. Depending on an almost semantic difference between a demand and a time deposit, estimates seem to vary between zero and one with the market therefore being the same or double the size of the stimulating deposits. Trying to estimate the magnitude of the Eurodollar market has also caused much heartache. Despite possibilities of double counting it is certainly of the order of $65 billion. This is enormous. It is for example larger than the domestic money supply of any single European country.

Short-term finance is provided in the form of direct Eurodollar loans. These are used for a variety of purposes such as the purchase of Eurodollar bonds, ordinary overdrafts, bridging finance or speculation. Most deposits are of less than one year, owing to the workings of the interest equalisation tax, but if banks have available longer-term money this they will relend. However, medium-term finance up to say eight years is now usually supplied in the form of roll-over loans. These loans are effectively made up of a succession of renewed short-term loans. Interest rates are also renewed at the same time and are usually calculated at some margin over London Inter-Bank rate say, $+\frac{3}{4}$ per cent to $+2$ per cent dependent on the security and standing of the borrowers. Loans are usually made on an unsecured basis if the borrower is sufficiently reputable. If not, either a parent company or bank guarantee may be called for, although the latter is usually expensive, perhaps 1 per cent per annum. There are no special exchange control regulations affecting only Eurodollars, but naturally operations are restrained by the national regulations currently in force. For example, while it is difficult for companies to indulge in short-term Eurodollar operations for end use in sterling, London banks operate quite freely in other currencies not so restricted by exchange control.

Bonds issued in a Eurocurrency, known as Eurobonds, are available with most of the usual variations, straight, convertible with warrants, etc. The first bond was issued in 1963 at a time when America's imposition of interest equalisation tax made debt raising in the States prohibitively expensive. Up to 1968 the market grew rapidly, but has since fallen off due to the turndown of US investment in Europe. The total loans now outstanding are of the order of \$10 billion; thus the Eurobond market is only about a sixth of the size of the Eurocurrency market. Bonds are at present usually denominated in dollars or Deutschmarks, and are issued by any borrower of sufficient standing, for example the larger corporations or national institutions such as local authorities. The funds are employed in most of the developed world outside the US, although one issue of \$15 million has been made to the Asian Development Bank. Bonds are generally placed privately by international syndicates of banks, the management of which is complex, and requires excellent contacts, and timing. The identity of the final lender is in fact often unknown to the public since many prefer to remain anonymous, if only to avoid tax. Most Eurobond interest is paid gross, which explains the trend of setting up special companies in tax havens from which to float such bonds. However, approximately 70 per cent of funds invested in the Eurobond market emanate from Switzerland, much of which is international flight money.

Once the bond has been sold, it can be quoted on a stock exchange in the usual way. However, while the Eurodollar market thrives on a lack of 'institutionalisation', the reverse is true of the Eurobond market, which suffers from being too narrow and volatile. One problem that arises is the lack of control over the timing of issues since the supply of funds to the market is fairly steady and an excess of new issues sometimes proves indigestible. A more important problem is the lack of an adequate secondary market, which results in investors being unable to sell their holdings freely. It is perhaps indicative that the most important stimulus to demand in the secondary market is still sinking-fund repurchases. There are two competing clearing systems, Euroclear in Brussels and Cedel in Luxembourg. Despite these facilities secondary market operations are still relatively unattractive. Commissions are much lower (about $\frac{1}{4}$ per cent compared with $1\frac{1}{2}$ per cent on new issues), there are no 'tombstone' advertisements as in the primary market, nor is there yet a sufficient infrastructure of suitable clients.

Overall, the development of the Eurodollar and Eurobond markets has been of great economic value. Its biggest contribution lies in its having reduced the chronic shortage of international liquidity, although this is not apparent in the usual comparisons of the growth of world trade with that of world reserves, since the Eurodollar represents only secondary liquidity. It has also permitted a much more flexible allocation of resources between countries, but this has had the inevitable result in a free enterprise system of shifting savings from the poorer to the richer countries. In some cases the richer countries have then reinvested the proceeds in the poorer, as has occurred with US investment in Europe. Further, by offering an alternative to local currencies it has made local credit markets more international, more efficient, and more interdependent. At the same time, the advent of the Eurodollar market has naturally brought with it some disadvantages apart from the inevitable increase in potential instability of any extension of international credit. By virtue of its huge size the Eurodollar market can have quite unwarranted external effects on a national economy which the local monetary authorities, trying to regulate their own money supply, are powerless to control. It is for this reason the Swiss restrict the convertibility of Eurobonds into Swiss francs. The Eurodollar market can thus greatly reduce an individual country's economic independence.* In

* An example of the lack of autonomy facing a national monetary authority is of course Germany, which having not only one of the freely convertible currencies in Europe, but also one that tends to be relatively overvalued, is peculiarly susceptible to external pressures. These take not only the usual speculative forms at any sign of a revaluation, but pose problems at the ordinary day-to-day level. For example, if the government wishes to control inflation, it would normally restrict the rate of growth of the money supply and let interest rates rise. In Germany's case, however, such a course of action merely makes Eurodollar loans more attractive, bearing in mind the mark revaluation possibilities, and industrialists switch their borrowing to this market, convert dollars back into marks on the free market and the cycle begins again, with no curb on inflation. Thus the Germans are not only unable to control their economy by monetary means, but the Bundesbank is embarrassed by its excess dollars. If on top of this

the extreme case the Eurodollar market also probably permitted the United States to continue to run a deficit longer than it could have otherwise, since commercial banks were content to hold such deficit dollars rather than flooding the central bank with them. It has also arrested the decline of London as an international banking centre. However, while initially operations were carried on mostly by British banks, branches of American banks now account for over 60 per cent of Eurodollar business in London. Thus, in spite of the market's taking business away from New York, it is more than compensated for by the increase in that city's international role.

Any discussion of the future of the Eurodollar market must take into account the fact that it is now an important source of international liquidity. Thus in the absence of acute protectionism, any serious attempt to destroy it, as is suggested by those who see it as a means of American takeover of Europe, will never succeed without first finding an effective substitute. In view of America's current overpowering economic strength, it is impossible to visualise any viable substitute that is not based on the dollar. This will be true even with the advent of European economic integration and a common currency, unless some quite startling changes take place in America's economic or political role in the world. Thus the repeal of Regulation 'Q', or the imposition of some much needed controls such as reserve requirements by the US and Germany and now possibly by Britain have had little long-term effect on the evolution of the market, other than to reduce its rate of growth. Another way of looking at this is to point to the steadily increasing demand provided by the large proportion of loans continually coming up for renewal plus new business. One much-discussed point is what will occur should the US run a consistent surplus sufficient to absorb the accumulated deficit that now supplies the market with its funds. No one can be certain of the answer, although one can hypothesise that the domestic dollar itself will again take on an increased role in world trade and international investment.

One may predict, therefore, that the Eurodollar market will continue to grow, but at nothing like the explosive rates seen in the sixties: at the same time it will become more institutionalised and controlled. All the same it would take a real optimist to prophesy the logical development, to wit the takeover of the Eurodollar's function by that of the Europa, EMU or what you will, controlled and issued by the Central Bank of Europe.

real speculation takes place, greatly facilitated by the funds available in the Eurodollar market, the maintenance of the mark parity can become impossible.

TOTAL GROSS DEPOSITS AT BANKS IN BRITAIN

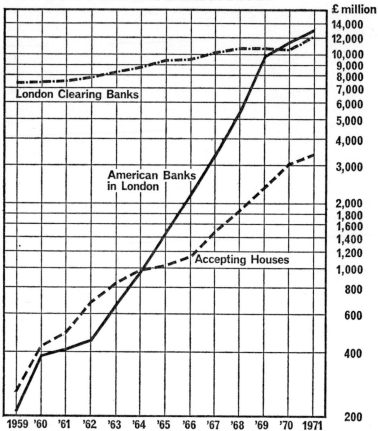

£ million

Source: Bank of England Quarterly Review.

Developments in European Banking

In the period immediately following the war European banks, with no shortage of deposits, found themselves in a lender's market. As a result they concentrated upon selling short-term finance to their industrial customers and made little attempt to cultivate deposits from the man in the street. These potential customers, deterred by the discouraging attitude of the banks, turned to the Giro systems for their current account needs and to the savings institutions for their deposit requirements. Thus substantial amounts of continental savings were channelled to institutions outside the commercial banking system. Initially this was of little importance but the end of the fifties brought a shift in the

33

requirements of industry which demanded increasingly longer-term facilities. In order to provide these, while maintaining an adequate liquidity structure, the banks found it necessary to seek time deposits and at the same time that they had to attract the savings of the private customers and the smaller companies which they had previously neglected. The result was increasing competition between the banks and the public sector. Facing a growing demand for funds from municipal and government authorities the savings institutions in particular strove to retain their share of the market by developing the services that hitherto only the banks had provided.

The increased competition for deposits coupled with the aggressive marketing policies copied from the American banks bred a sophistication in the client that only exacerbated the situation. Not only was he no longer prepared to leave funds on current account but he was also not prepared to continue a relationship merely because it was of long standing. Today he seeks the best terms and will shop around for them. As the range of services was broadened to provide an adequate marketing base the distinctions between the various institutions began to break down. Government legislation such as that in the Netherlands only accelerated the trend by recognising and formalising the changes that market forces had brought about; in France legislation created it. The outcome has been comprehensive department store banking. This process is perhaps most developed in Germany, where, despite differences of history, most banks now offer most services. In Britain, at the other extreme, specialisation is still the order of the day.

Those least able to resist such competition have been the small private banks whose position has greatly deteriorated with many being forced to sell out or merge. The specialised services that had once been their monopoly became the common property of many of the savings institutions and the general banks. At the same time their corporate customers demanded increased credit facilities. Poorly placed to obtain deposits and dependent on a lending capability to attract and retain worthwhile custom, the small banks faced a serious challenge to their continued existence as viable independent units. Their initial response was to fall back on the nebulous defences of flexibility and personal service. These, however, proved insufficient and diversification was required. To some, this was impossible; a few, such as Banque Rothschild, have opened branches in order to attract more deposits but many would argue that the overheads involved make such deposits prohibitively expensive; some have increased their specialisation or diversified into such sophisticated fields as international investment advice, leasing or factoring; others have seen a wider geographic field of operation as the answer and, like Banque Suez, have linked up with similar institutions abroad. Another variant that may well point to a future trend is for private banks to enter into joint operations with savings institutions—providing badly required expertise in return for an entrée to the deposits. The recent establishment of a central Dutch savings institution, along the lines of a German Girozentrale, by Bank Mees & Hope with the ubiquitous Westdeutsche Landesbank is an interesting example.

In general it is clear that the smaller banks face a period of greater difficulty despite these tactical diversifications. One French bank even went so far as to say that it may not be in business in ten years, and others, if less explicit, are prey to similar fears. For the problem remains: if they are small enough to be truly flexible and personal they are almost certainly too small to satisfy their major customers' requirements. If they are large enough to do so they tend to lose their special characteristics and come into even closer competition with the larger banks compared with which they are at a serious disadvantage. Furthermore, there is a growing concern at the apparently decreasing desire of corporations to pay for the personal touch. The future will certainly bring further amalgamations and takeovers. The disagreeable truth may well be that, unless the majority of private banks can come up with some new formula to justify their continued existence, many will cease to remain independent. One may well ask whether there is a lesson here for the London merchant banks.

At the national level, the fifties and sixties were a period of fundamental change out of which comprehensive banking has emerged. Though much of the personal style may have been lost there is little doubt that, from the corporate customers' point of view, there has been an improvement in the range and quality of the services offered. Further diversification of service and concentration of power may be expected though at a reduced pace. However, for major developments one should look to the international sphere where the lines have been drawn but serious battle is yet to commence.

The decade which saw radical changes at the national level also witnessed two significant developments in the international sphere. The first was the establishment of a number of medium-term Eurocurrency lending consortia. The second of these was the establishment of four major bank groupings* which aimed to provide a comprehensive

* ORION; SFE; CCB; EBIC.
Members as follows:
ORION: Chase Manhattan, Royal Bank of Canada, Westdeutsche Landesbank Girozentrale, National Westminster, Credito Italiano, Mitsubishi Bank.

international banking service. It is too early to say whether the former, which have been formed partly to facilitate the offering of particular forms of credit, and partly through fashion, have any long-term significance; however the latter development, although still at the embryonic stage, may well prove to be of great importance. It not only has implications for the banking system as a whole but it also exemplifies the sort of cross-national arrangement dear to the hearts of the founding fathers of the European Community.

Within the financial Community there is much speculation as to the philosophy underlying these groupings and their probable chances of success. While it is apparent that the development of the EEC had little direct influence on their emergence it is difficult to identify any common rationale behind their formation. However, four major reasons are usually put forward. The most frequently cited is the need to counter the increased competition of the major American (and Japanese) banks whose European branch networks, cash management schemes and world-wide organisation were felt to pose a serious threat to the European banks, already engaged in fierce domestic competition. Either an offensive and defensive European alliance could be formed as a remedy, such as EBIC and CCB, or the US banks could be drawn into alliance, as in the case of ORION or SFE. It seems, however, that the increased American presence was a psychological, rather than a commercial consideration, since it is now known that, after an initial honeymoon period of preferential rates, European companies have tended to return to their national banks. Nevertheless, anyone who has experienced the European paranoia over American incursions cannot discard it as a contributory factor. Rather, it seems that the US banks involved, whose profitability is said to have been disappointing, sought allies in Europe and an entrée into local deposits—perhaps the clearest rebuttal of the *Défi Americain* argument.

A further case put forward is the belief that the size of the bank should match the size of the customer. It is worth noting, however, that many, such as the UK merchant banks, consider that size itself is not of prime importance. They place greater emphasis upon ability to mobilise funds when required. Others consider that the search for size is a dangerous shibboleth and point out that, except for shared overseas

SFE (Société Financière Européenne): Dresdner Bank, Bayerische Hypotheken und Wechselbank, Algemene Bank Nederland, Banque de Bruxelles, Bank of America, Barclays, Banca Nazionale del Lavoro, Banque Nationale de Paris.
CCB: Credit Lyonnais, Commerzbank, Banco di Roma.
EBIC (European Banks International Company): Midland, Amsterdam-Rotterdam, Deutsche Bank, Société Générale, Société Générale de Banque, Creditanstalt Bankverein.

costs, there are few economies of scale involved. Furthermore, the attention which large companies give to the rates they are prepared to pay tends to offset the reduced risk and consequently such business can affect margins unfavourably. Justified or not, however, the search for size was certainly an influencing factor.

The need for a wider geographic spread to match that of industrial companies expanding abroad is also held out as a rationale. Unlike the major US banks, who achieved this by the expanding of their own branch network, the European banks preferred consortia—despite the loss of independence involved. This was probably because few have a sufficient portfolio of international companies to justify going it alone. It has yet to be proved, however, that joint venture offers significantly greater benefits than the old 'most favoured correspondent' system. As an example of the sorts of problems involved, it is said that Algemene Nederland is resisting Dresdner Bank's desire to utilise its widespread overseas network. From the point of view of ultimate merger, however —of which much loose talk is heard—there can be little doubt that joint overseas operations, such as EBIC's European American banking Corporation, provide a good method of getting to know one another prior to any marriage.

A final contributory factor not to be overlooked was mere fashion-following. No one, for obvious reasons, will admit it about themselves, but there is no doubt that amidst all the talk about the EEC and the popularity of international co-operation some banks joined consortia out of misplaced optimism. Others, seeing the trend and joining in order not to be left out, found that their partners had been chosen for them by the course of events.

Representatives of the twenty banks involved like to point to one or other of these factors as the major rationale behind their decision to join a consortium. It is probable that all four played a part. In view of the contradictory statements one hears, one may question the precision with which any bank could at the outset have formulated its specific objectives or the strategy necessary to achieve them. Post facto rationalisation is certainly at work. Whatever the reasons, the results are the foundations of what will possibly emerge as the first real European banks.

Chapter Four

The French Financial System

In France government institutions dominate the workings of the financial markets. It has been estimated that approximately 80 per cent of all medium- and long-term finance passes at some stage through government hands and it is not surprising therefore that William François, writing on the concept of capital in France, entitled his book *Le Capital sans Capitalisme*. Although French financiers may admire the way in which the City plays its markets just as they do the horses, many of them are doubtful whether there is a place for bookmakers in a country such as theirs where there is already an effective 'Tote' in the form of government agencies.

The French authorities have for some time been aware of certain deficiencies in their financial system. Many commentators have, for example, attributed the low rate of investment of the mid-sixties to the difficulty of mobilising and allocating the necessary capital and a succession of committees has been established to report on various aspects of the capital market and its institutions. One of the most influential studies was that of the Lorain Committee in 1963 which analysed the structure of the capital market. More recently the Baumgartner Commission reported on the equity market, and while this Report has led to conjecture abroad that the French Bourse might live up to the first word of the motto emblazoned on its exterior—'Liberté, Fraternité, Egalité'—Paris brokers are less optimistic.

Despite the constant flow of recommendations from such committees, which have all tended to recommend that Paris should be more market-orientated, it seems that it will take more than technical innovations and tax incentives to alter either the structure of the financial institutions or the marked liquidity preference of French savers, both of which have their roots deep in French history and tradition. It is not merely institutions but attitudes that will have to change. The average French individual's approach to finance may be difficult for an Anglo-Saxon to understand, but seen against the background of France's economy, with years of inflation and successive devaluations, it becomes more comprehensible. The decade of Gaullist prosperity and stability is seen, probably correctly, as a mere interlude that does nothing to invalidate the Frenchman's basic view that short-term investments should be held in near cash and be readily realisable while long-term funds should be safely secreted in real estate. In seeking a justification for this view it is only necessary to consider the success with which fortunes have been preserved from the ravages of time and the 'Fisc' (the French Inland Revenue). Post-war nationalisations and the poor performance of the Bourse before spring 1972 only tended to confirm the belief that equity investment was a dangerous gamble and an almost certain loser. Since the great majority of French companies are small family concerns primarily orientated around the preservation of family fortunes it is hardly surprising that their style of management has reflected not a desire to grow and prosper but a desire to conserve and secure the families' assets.

The whole character of the financial scene is dominated by this concept of preservation. Broadly, assets are purchased to be held, dealing is left to a few professional institutions and savings are invested at short-term. Within this framework successive governments have found it necessary to establish their own institutions to offer the services that the private sector could not or would not provide, with the result that the tentacles of government reach far into every corner of daily business.

Savings

The importance of household savings in financing France's economic growth was well summed up in a report of the Commission des Opérations de Bourse:

'Dans les pays modernes, la plupart des agents économiques épargnent d'une façon ou d'une autre, mais du moins en France de toutes les formes d'épargne celle des particuliers est pratiquement la seule à alimenter le marché financier en capitaux nouveaux que ce soit directement ou par l'intermédiaire des institutions qui collectent cette épargne (banques, caisses d'épargne, compagnies d'assurances etc). Tous les autres agents économiques affectent la totalité de leur épargne au financement de leurs investissements et comme celle-ci est généralement insuffisante se retrouvent emprunteurs sur le marché des capitaux.'

The household sector has on average accounted for over 40 per cent of total gross savings over the past five years and has been the most important source of new capital for industry (see table 1). The problem is that only a very small proportion of these funds are in a form which industry can make use of directly, as the private saver keeps most of his savings in cash or short-term deposits with the banks and savings institutions. Indeed the government has granted various tax exemptions, which have made the return from certain liquid savings more attractive than other long-term investments. The figures in table 2 highlight this;

Table 1: Gross Savings in Millions of Francs

	1967	1968	1969	1970	1971
TOTAL GROSS SAVINGS	146,843	159,436	198,789	231,114	246,692
of which:	%	%	%	%	%
Households	43	42	37	41	42
Private Enterprises	24	27	29	27	28
Public Authorities	13	11	15	15	13
Public Enterprises	14	14	12	11	10
Financial Institutions	5	6	7	5	6

Source: Rapport sur les Comptes de la Nation 1971.

Table 2: Savers' Holdings of Selected Assets in %

	1967	1968	1969	1970	1971
	%	%	%	%	%
Housing	34	36	41	33	34
Currency	6	13	0	13	12
Various forms of Deposits	31	18	28	26	28
Life Insurance	2	2	2	2	2
Securities	7	5	6	2	7
Other	20	26	24	24	18

Source: Rapport sur les Comptes de la Nation 1971.

in 1971 only 7 per cent of household savings was committed to security purchases and only 2 per cent to life insurance. The burden of converting the remaining essentially short-term funds into the long-term finance required by industry falls on a range of financial intermediaries comprising not only the banks but also public and para-public institutions (see table 3). A large volume of short-term funds is converted into medium- and long-term finance for industry but many people still consider that the supply remains insufficient.

The aim of government measures over the past decade has been to facilitate the transformation process. Banking regulations have been modified to allow commercial banks to accept savings deposits for periods longer than two years, previously the maximum. Interest rate structures and fiscal regulations have been amended in an effort to make longer-term saving more attractive to savers.

Table 3: Transformation Process in Millions of Francs

	1969	1970	1971
Short-term Resources	41,000	69,500	78,000
Long-term Resources	30,000	37,000	40,000
Short-term Loans	6,000	43,000	45,000
Medium or Long-term Loans and Securities	65,000	63,000	73,500

Source: Rapport sur les Comptes de la Nation 1971.

Investment

Gross investment in France has increased by an average of 7 per cent p.a. since 1959. During the early sixties much of this growth took place in the public sector but from 1967 the private sector improved. Public sector investment now runs at about a quarter of the investment of private companies (see table 4). Recently investment has tended to slow

Table 4: Gross Investment by Sector in Billions of Francs

	1967	1968	1969	1970	1971
Productive Investment of which:	84	91	108	126	141
Public Enterprises	22	23	24	27	28
Private Enterprises	62	68	84	99	113
Investment in Housing of which:	39	44	49	54	60
Enterprises	10	12	13	14	14
Households	29	32	36	40	46
Other Investments	20	22	25	28	30
TOTAL	144	158	183	208	231
% Increase in Volume	6·9	6·9	9·2	6·4	5·8
% Increase in Value	9·6	9·7	15·8	13·7	11·1

Source: Rapport sur les Comptes de la Nation 1971.

down, partly caused by the high level of capital formation by companies in 1969 and 1970 and partly as a result of an overall decline in business confidence.

Company Finance

As can be seen from Table 5 the self-financing ratio of both public and private enterprises has been high over the past five years. In recent years the private sector has been forced to seek increasing external finance due to narrower profit margins and perhaps also to rapid expansion in many sectors although finance has not always been widely available at the longer end of the market. In the early sixties by contrast the nationalised

Table 5: Sources of Finance for Nationalised and Private Industry

Nationalised Sector

	1967	*1968*	*1969*	*1970*	*1971*
TOTAL, F.F. Millions	32·946	36·032	38·866	38·896	—
Savings	63%	61%	63%	66%	—
Medium- and Long-term Loans and Capital Market	39%	35%	34%	33%	—
Short-term Credit	−2%	4%	3%	1%	—
Rate of Self-financing	67%	68%	72%	72%	70%

Private Sector

	1967	*1968*	*1969*	*1970*	*1971*
TOTAL, F.F. Millions	60·442	73·203	88·742	120·128	—
Savings	62%	60%	68%	55%	—
Medium- and Long-term Loans and Capital Market	17%	13%	23%	20%	—
Short-term Credit	21%	26%	9%	25%	—
Rate of Self-financing	73%	80%	68%	66%	68%

Source: Rapport sur les Comptes de la Nation 1971.

industries, operating on low profit margins, were only able to finance 25 per cent of their investment needs from internal sources making them highly dependent on loans from financial institutions and on the capital market to which they were given privileged access by the Treasury; urban renewal programmes also made heavy calls for long-term finance and as a result private industry had some difficulty financing its needs. The situation has changed during the past five years but even today it is interesting to note that well over 30 per cent of nationalised industries' needs are filled by long-term loans and capital market issues, whereas only about 20 per cent of private industries' needs are met this way (see table 5). Possibly as a result of their difficulty in obtaining longer-term funds, private industry has relied on cheaper short-term credit supplied mainly by the banks and specialised credit institutions. But in order for public companies to maintain reasonable debt–equity ratios, new equity issues have been frequent and total volume compares very favourably with other countries, though as a result of the weakness of the market, issues have been costly (see table 6).

Table 6: Issues of Shares as % of GNP

	1969	1970
France	1·08	1·06
Japan	0·91	1·45
USA	0·89	0·87
Germany	0·46	0·53
UK	0·45	0·15

Source: Commission des Operations de Bourse.

Financial Institutions

The French financial market can be crudely divided into three broad categories of institutions. Firstly there are those which collect the liquid savings of private individuals and transform them into productive investment; these comprise certain public and semi-public institutions such as the Crédit Agricole, the Caisses d'Épargne with their central government agency, the Caisse des Dépôts et de Consignations and the equivalent of our clearing banks known as Banques de Dépôts. The second broad category embraces those semi-public institutions such as the Crédit National and Crédit Foncier which enter the capital market and compete with other borrowers for long-term funds. The third category includes such institutions as the insurance companies and the unit trusts or SICAVs which channel the funds they collect into the capital market. There is little distinction between the first two categories —the Crédit Agricole for example is a major operator on the capital market—but this separation of functions may be of some assistance in clarifying the pattern of French institutions which can be confusing to an outsider.

Savings and Credit Institutions

The public and para-public institutions dominate the collection of liquid savings, taking about 85 per cent of France's total deposits which in 1970 amounted to 390 billion francs. Of this 85 per cent, almost 30 per cent is deposited with the 4,000 branches of the Caisse d'Épargne and the Caisse Nationale d'Épargne (postal savings system). These savings, except for a small reserve retained in the individual savings banks, are all channelled to the Caisse des Dépôts et de Consignations, a government agency situated in Paris. This institution is the largest in France; not merely does it manage all the Caisses d'Épargne funds but also those of certain pension funds and a life assurance company owned by the Caisse des Dépôts itself. It is estimated that in 1973 it will handle 175 billion French francs, a sum roughly equivalent to the annual budget of the State and larger than the market capitalisation of the Bourse.

The Caisse des Dépôts was established 150 years ago to guarantee the national debt and although responsible to Parliament rather than to the Ministère des Finances, it is not surprising to find that it is the chief source of finance for the public sector. In fact the Caisse des Dépôts allocates its resources fairly evenly between three sectors—finance for local authorities, finance for low-cost housing and investment in the capital market, retaining a 20 per cent liquidity reserve. The power and influence of the Caisse des Dépôts in the equity and bond markets cannot be over-estimated for it is not merely a major buyer of shares but also accounts for 16 per cent of the placing power in the bond market. The Caisse generally plays a passive role and rarely intervenes in the management of those companies in which it has major interests, but despite this, it can find itself in a key position when it comes to takeovers and in one or two of the major battles of recent years the Caisse has played a major role. Its activities on the capital market have earned it the reputation of controlling and even regulating both bond and equity markets. It also has subsidiaries carrying out other activities ranging from the management of three SICAVs worth 3·5 billion francs to the provision of consultancy services for the construction industry.

The other major institution, with a 15 per cent share of liquid savings, is the para-public Crédit Agricole, France's largest bank, which has a network of 7,000 branches spread throughout the countryside with the

Caisse Nationale de Crédit Agricole as its central bank. Its funds, which are augmented by borrowing on the capital market, have by law to be channelled to users whose activities are agricultural or rural but it has recently upset the commercial banks by opening a new branch in the heart of Paris. More disturbing still to its competitors has been the Crédit Agricole's success in attracting savings and in competing directly with them in extending loans to and taking equity participations in the food-processing industry. This is clearly an industry which falls within the Crédit Agricole's agricultural preserve but if the progress of the farmers' co-operative banks in Holland and the credit co-operatives in Germany is anything to go by it will be surprising if the Crédit Agricole does not penetrate further into traditional spheres of banking, accepting a loss of certain privileges for a change in its statutes.

The Crédit Agricole's ability to offer loans on favourable terms has caused considerable alarm amongst its commercial bank competitors who in total account for a further 42 per cent of liquid savings. Of this nearly two-thirds is accounted for by the three big nationalised banks, the Banque Nationale de Paris, the Crédit Lyonnais and the Société Générale. Their nearest rival is the Crédit Industriel et Commercial (with an estimated 10 per cent of bank deposits) which has finally been taken over by the Banque de Suez et de l'Union des Mines after a lengthy battle with the Banque de Paris et des Pays Bas.

These two Banques d'Affaires, the largest in France, have been extremely active in establishing a commercial banking network following the 1967 change in the banking laws which abolished the traditional distinction between Banques de Dépôts and Banques d'Affaires. In return for ceding its 30 per cent interest in Crédit Industriel et Commercial to Suez, Parisbas received the Suez majority holding in Banque de l'Union Parisienne to complement its own clearing bank network, the sixth largest in France, and its stake in Crédit du Nord. Thus the two Banques d'Affaires have both established large commercial bank networks leaving only the Crédit Commercial de France as an eligible private clearing bank for hungry bidders, for Suez has recently acquired the other candidate for takeover, the Banque de l'Indochine.

Seventy per cent of commercial bank deposits are demand or short-term deposits and the banks are correspondingly active in short-term credit, most of which takes the form of discounted trade bills which can be refinanced with the Banque de France. It is through manipulation of these rediscount facilities that the Central Bank exerts a powerful control over bank lending. Each bank has a ceiling on the total amount it can rediscount at the official bank rate and the banks can only exceed these at the expense of a higher discount rate. But the discounting system is lengthy and cumbersome, involving an enormous amount of paper-work, and the much simpler overdraft is now becoming more popular.

Commercial banks are also active in granting medium-term loans for up to seven years to finance industrial expansion and modernisation. The main problem has been the short-term nature of their deposits but the banks have been able to overcome this difficulty by rediscounting such loans if they are approved by the Crédit National. The dangers of lending long from these short-term resources induced the authorities in 1965 to remove the restriction which had formerly forbidden the banks to accept fixed deposits of longer than two years. This has meant that a much larger proportion of their medium-term loans have been backed by the banks' own longer-term resources and in turn has increased the flow of savings into longer-term investment.

The commercial banks also play a vital role in the capital market by underwriting and placing issues of securities. New issues are placed with clients through their branch networks, which have also assisted them in playing the major role in the development of the SICAVs which are almost exclusively bank managed, the exceptions being those run by the Caisse des Dépôts and insurance companies.

Before passing on to the institutions which borrow on the capital market, it is worth briefly touching on the role of the Banques d'Affaires, which have often been likened to the British merchant banks. There are however major differences. Merchant banks have been able to take enormous advantage of the London Stock Market and while Banques d'Affaires do offer comparable services these are less developed. In fact many banks are no more than financial holding companies having more in common with the newer financial conglomerate than a traditional British merchant bank. The Parisbas and Suez groups own the two largest Banques d'Affaires and it is interesting to note that the British government and INA Corporation have substantial participations in the latter. The complicated history and structure of these two holding companies is difficult to unravel but both now have important banking and industrial networks. As we have seen, these networks have recently been extended and provide a wide range of services including equity-orientated activities such as advice on mergers and acquisitions, management of investment portfolios and new issues business; they also have considerable interests in a number of foreign banking and insurance institutions. Their industrial tentacles extend into a many sectors; Suez has considerable interest in the merged St Gobain-Pont-à-Mousson and at least fifteen other major participations in companies ranging from oil to the car industry. Parisbas's interests include participations in important oil, mining and chemical companies as well as interests in printing and electrical engineering. These banks often play an active part in the management of the companies in which they have holdings and the size of the participation does not necessarily reflect the extent of their management involvement.

Out of the big league there are a number of smaller, mostly private, Banques d'Affaires. Amongst the better known are: Banque Worms; Lazard Frères; Banque Louis Dreyfus; de Neuflize, Schlumberger, Mallet and Banque Rothschild. Some of these have traditional interests in particular areas, such as Worms in shipping and Dreyfus in wheat, and control major family interests in a wide variety of industries. In 1971 Parisbas attempted to take over de Neuflize, which had suffered a severe setback following the default of a major creditor, the property company Patrimoine Foncier, whose financial director had fled the country. Although the bid failed a major stake in de Neuflize has now been taken by the Dutch Bank Mees & Hope, in which it is interesting to note that Morgan Guarranty has a 20 per cent holding.

On the whole, however, the main structure of French banking seems unlikely to alter very much in the foreseeable future. The big Banques d'Affaires have sorted out their commercial banking interests and the smaller Banque d'Affaires will remain active in their specialist areas. No threat is possible to the domination of the big three nationalised banks, though competition seems bound to increase at the retail banking level.

Financial Institutions which Concentrate on the Capital Market

The Crédit National is as important on the financial market as the Caisse des Dépôts, for not merely does it provide the banks with rediscount facilities for loans which it has approved but is also itself the main source of long-term loans to industry. Although its senior managers are appointed by the government and loans are generally allocated on the basis of national interest outlined in the national plan, applications for loans are often considered by a consultative Committee of over thirty of the most important businessmen in key industrial sectors. It is not itself allowed to take deposits from the public but raises most of its funds by sales of its own bonds in the capital market; substantial sums are also borrowed from the insurance companies and the Caisse des Dépôts.

There are many other specialised institutions which borrow money on the capital market to lend on for specific purposes. The Crédit Foncier specialises in mortgage loans though it does not make loans for industrial buildings. The Crédit Hotelier has also issued bonds on the market to finance hotel construction. The Caisse Nationale des Marchés de l'Etat is another government agency which facilitates the financing of projects under government contract by providing an endorsement on medium-term loans thus making them eligible for rediscount at the Crédit National. Another group of institutions which raises capital through bond issues on the market are the regional development banks (Sociétés de Développement Régional) which finance local projects by extending medium- and long-term loans.

This brief description of the major operators in the financial markets underlines the point made at the beginning of this chapter concerning the role and influence of publicly owned institutions. Under these circumstances it is easy to overlook the intense competition which exists between some of them and between the BNP, Crédit Lyonnais and Société Générale which only tends to lessen when outsiders threaten their position—as the foreign banks in Paris discovered in the early part of 1972. The French banks, upset at the foreign banks' operations in the money market, kept out of it for a couple of days. Overnight rates more than doubled to 9 per cent and one American bank had to go to the Crédit Agricole for US $10 million; this action was clearly intended as a gentle warning to the foreign intruders to watch their step. In general however the system works remarkably well and although in many ways it is as if the Civil Service were to run the City, it is important to realise that just because it is different does not mean it is less effective.

Insurance Companies, Unit Trusts and Pension Funds

Household savings are not merely channelled to a capital market by the financial intermediaries and by private individuals' direct purchases of bonds and shares but also by institutional investors such as the insurance companies and unit trusts. Insurance companies in France, of which there are some 450, have played a far less important role than they have in other countries. Life assurance has not been popular with investors, partly as a result of the activities of the Sécurité Sociale and also for reasons of inflation, and in 1971 it accounted for only 2 per cent of total savings. French insurance companies are subject to strict controls regarding the investment of their technical reserves, although these rules are at this moment being reviewed. At present at least 50 per cent of their technical reserves must be in government securities or bonds of the nationalised industries but it is planned to suppress the distinction between government and industrial fixed interest securities and to allow insurance companies to make direct loans to industry. To what extent this latter innovation will make any difference is difficult to tell but few insurers feel that the envisaged relaxation of the rules will result in a substantially greater volume of funds being invested in equities. The investment portfolio of life insurance companies in 1969 is shown in table 7. Another important rule from which insurers suffer is that reserves must be held in the currency of the risks they cover to obviate the exchange risk.

Table 7: Portfolio of Life Insurance Companies in %

	1969
Public Sector Bonds	54
Private Sector Bonds	7
French Equities	22
Foreign and Non-Quoted Equities	10

Source: Le Capital sans Capitalisme, William François (Editions Fayard).

SICAVs (Sociétés d'Investissement à Capital Variable) were founded by the banks in the early sixties and took the form of open-ended investment trusts. After a somewhat slow start, partly due to the weakness of the Bourse and also to the IOS debacle, the number of trusts has risen from nine in 1965 to sixty-three at the end of 1971 and the total funds from 910 million francs in 1965 to 16 billion francs in 1971. The vast majority of the units on offer are sold through bank branches throughout the country which gives the banks virtual control of the market since the methods of sale of SICAV units is considerably more restricted than in Britain. Insurance companies have recently introduced SICAV-linked life policies, though it is too soon to judge their impact. SICAVs have brought an average of 3 billion francs to the capital market every year for the past three years. There is a wide variety of specialisation; twelve of the sixty-three are almost entirely invested in fixed interest securities—four are in property and the remaining forty-seven in a mixture of French and foreign securities. However, bond purchases account for 60 per cent of the total and while 1971 may have been an exceptional year because of the extremely high bond interest rates (with as much as 73 per cent of total acquisitions being in bonds), this left a mere 7 per cent invested in French equities, while 20 per cent was placed in foreign securities (see table 8). This state of affairs clearly did little to help the Bourse which in fact saw less trading in 1971 than 1970. The SICAVs are subject to certain investment rules: 90 per cent of their capital must be in quoted securities and they can hold no more than 5 per cent of the equity of any one company. In addition at least

30 per cent of their investments must be in bonds or liquid assets but as can be seen from table 8 this has been no restriction; in fact the Ministry of Finance has recently been approached to abolish the rule, in order to give investment companies greater freedom and flexibility.

Closed-end investment trusts (Société d'Investissement Fermé) have not had any great public success and are largely in the hands of the financial groups which founded them. They are forbidden to gear themselves up and were largely formed for tax reasons. The majority of the

Table 8: Investments of the SICAVs in Millions of Francs

	1970	%	1971	%
Portfolio	11,994	91·6	15,366	93·4
French Equities	2,975		3,225	
Foreign Equities	2,088		2,820	
French Bonds	6,653		9,111	
Foreign Bonds	278		210	
Liquid Funds	1,102	8·4	1,091	6·6
	13,096	100	16,457	100

Source: Commission des Operations de Bourse.

private pension funds in France are not funded, meeting benefit payments out of current income from contributions and therefore have little in the way of reserves for investment. The greater part of all pensions are, in any event, provided by the government's own scheme.

The Bond and Equity Markets

Table 9 reveals that new issues totalled 32 billion francs in 1971. This sum, however, only totalled 11·4 per cent of the funds needed to finance gross investment in 1971, an advance on the two previous years when the percentages were respectively 9 and 8 per cent. These figures are approximately equivalent to those for Germany and Britain but fall way behind the US and Japan where in 1970 42 and 14 per cent respectively of gross investment was financed through the capital market (see table 10).

Private industry is by no means totally dependent on the public sector for its finance. Substantial amounts of capital are raised through the equity markets (Tables 6 and 10) and French equity issues compare favourably with those of other major industrial countries. Many of these

Table 9: New Issues in Millions of Francs

| | 1970 | | | | 1971 | | | |
	Shares	%	Bonds	%	Shares	%	Bonds	%
Public Enterprises	—	—	3,615	21	—	—	5,388	21
Private Enterprises	5,130	64	4,013	23	5,058	69	6,600	26
Public and Semi-Public Financial Institutions	95	1	8,300	47	8	0	9,431	38
Private Financial Institutions	2,842	35	316	2	2,305	31	1,673	7
State and Local Authorities	—	—	1,073	6	—	—	1,703	7
Foreign	18	0	231	1	4	0	330	1
TOTAL	8,085	100	17,548	100	7,375	100	25,125	100

Source: Rapport sur les Comptes de la Nation 1971.

issues take the form of rights issues to existing shareholders and there is considerable pressure on French companies to come to the market fairly frequently in order to maintain a reasonable balance between equity and debt in their capital structures.

The bond market is dominated by the annual issues of public credit institutions and nationalised industries; approximately half of the bonds issued by this sector are those of the Crédit Agricole and the Crédit Foncier. The authorities operate a queue system; private companies wishing to issue bonds have to inform the Treasury, which draws up a timetable designed to favour the public sector. This often means that private companies suffer severe delays. In fact it is only large private companies which come to the bond market on their own, and in 1971 fourteen such companies accounted for over 40 per cent of the total funds raised by the private sector. Other companies come to the market as members of a group of firms in the same industry joining together to raise capital. This unique feature of the French market enables medium-sized companies to raise bond finance. A similar principle applies in the case of the regional development banks which raise capital on behalf of quoted and non-quoted companies and pass on the proceeds in the form of loans. There were eleven group issues in 1971 totalling 2·6 billion francs and a total of 571 companies received finance which had been raised either through group issues (198 companies) or through regional bank issues (373 companies).* Needless to say, an even greater number of companies benefited from the loans of the Crédit National and the other nationalised credit institutions which had also raised their funds on the bond market.

Underwriting and placing is usually undertaken by a syndicate of bankers who either place stock with institutions or sell it through their branch networks to the public. The SICAVs acquired over 9 billion francs' worth of bonds during 1971 and the insurance companies, for whom a portion of new issues are reserved, took up a further 3 billion francs' worth. Bond issues accounted for over 77 per cent of the new capital brought to the market in 1971 and issues were often oversubscribed.

There has been much criticism of the French equity market over the last decade and in March 1971 the Ministère des Finances set up a Commission under M. Baumgartner to suggest ways of revitalising it. Before examining the various measures that his Commission and others have proposed, it is worth looking in detail at the structure of the Bourse.

The most obvious characteristic of the French equity market is that it

* *Source:* Report of the Commisson des Operations de Bourse.

Table 10: Issues of Securities as a % of Gross Investment

SHARES				BONDS				TOTAL			
1969		1970		1969		1970		1969		1970	
USA	6	USA	6	USA	18	USA	36	USA	24	USA	42
France	4	France	4	Japan	11	Japan	10	Japan	14	Japan	14
Japan	3	Japan	4	Germany	10	Germany	8	Germany	12	Germany	10
UK	2·5	Germany	2	UK	7	UK	7	UK	9·5	France	9
Germany	2	UK	1	France	3	France	5	France	7	UK	8

Source: Commission des Operations de Bourse.

is deprived of the large volume of funds which feed Anglo-Saxon equity markets.

Private individuals have not been particularly attracted to the market and have not been encouraged to buy shares by their banks. Indeed a recent survey has shown that the share of fixed interest securities in private portfolios has risen from 25 to 33 per cent between 1966 and 1970. But it is not merely private individuals but also the institutions who have shied away from the equity markets. Even the SICAVs which it was believed would give a considerable boost to the equity market now have three times as much invested in bonds as in domestic equities. There are numerous reasons for this lack of investor interest. French companies are loath to provide investors with adequate and up-to-date information about their activities, although the situation is improving. The problems that French companies seeking quotations in London have faced in reaching the accounting standards required by the Stock Exchange demonstrate the quality of the information available to French shareholders. Another cause for wariness is that the bulk of the shares of many firms are held by the Banques d'Affaires, families, and the Caisse des Dépôts and are rarely traded; the market is therefore very narrow and about 50 per cent of trading is carried out in a mere fifty shares. In such a market, prices tend to be volatile. Furthermore the major shareholders often have access to supplementary information. To the public at large, therefore, the equity market is a closed shop. One commercial banker commented, 'Les grandes affaires jouent au football entre eux.' Nowhere is this evidenced more clearly than in the field of takeovers, which tend to resemble exercises in game-theory between powerful interests and Banques d'Affaires, often resulting in stalemate. Public takeovers, which are hampered by the fact that most shares are in bearer form, are regarded with disfavour and success is improbable except when bids are agreed between the parties.

Despite the weaknesses of the secondary trading market, French companies have issued large amounts of share capital though this has tended to be a costly method of finance due to the level of the discount normally required to guarantee success. This of course has undesirable consequences for the companies as well as for the shareholders as it results in dilution of the company's capital and the numerous rights issues have also had a persistent weakening effect on the market.

There are seven stock exchanges in France. Paris is by far the most important, with a market capitalisation at the end of 1971 of £9·3 billion and approximately 830 quoted companies. There are some sixty-three Agents de Change or stockbrokers, government appointees with unlimited personal liability whose Association manages a compensation fund to protect clients. They have a monopoly of transactions, though 'personnes physiques', private individuals, may deal outside the market. There are no jobbers and most deals are matched mathematically at the Premier Cours, the first market session.

There are two distinct markets, the Marché au Comptant (cash market), where transactions have to be settled within four days, and the more important Marché à Terme for larger companies only where accounts are for monthly settlement. The market is open every weekday from 12.30 to 2.30 p.m. and there is no official dealing outside these hours, or indeed outside the Bourse, although unofficial dealing is permitted between the previous day's bid and offer prices. Daily price changes of more than 5 per cent are not permitted and should they occur the share is suspended to permit possible buyers or sellers to reconsider their position. Brokers consider that their delivery system (SICOVAM), like that of the Germans, was superior to London's but it does depend on the shares being in bearer as opposed to registered form.

The mechanisms of the French equity market are far less flexible than those of London, and the recent Baumgartner recommendations have been directed not only to increasing the flow of the funds to the market but also to improving its mechanisms. These reforms have been prompted as much by fears of what will happen to the equity market in an enlarged EEC as by the dissatisfaction of operators. In fact it is difficult to believe that the authorities are interested in increasing the role of the equity market since an increase in its importance as a primary market would tend to diminish their grip on the nation's finances. On the other hand failure to reinforce the Bourse might result in a severe weakening of Paris as an international centre with, ultimately, French companies seeking funds elsewhere. The 1971 Report of the Commission des Operations de Bourse summed up French fears: 'Les sociétés savent déjà et sauront mieux encore dans un avenir plus proche comparer les mérites respectifs des divers marchés de capitaux. Lorsqu'elles seront cotées sur plusieurs bourses, le marché principal de leurs actions pourrait fort bien se déplacer.' A number of French companies are already seeking quotations in London, though it is difficult to see at the moment how this can be much more than a public relations exercise. Activity on the French Bourse itself has considerably increased during 1972, largely the result of foreign institutional buying. Indeed daily turnover increased from an average of 150 million francs per day during 1971 to over 300 million francs per day in 1972. To foreign institutions the shares of French companies look very cheap just as they did to American buyers at the beginning of the sixties when prices were forced up until they bore little relation to the profitability of the respective companies. Gradually prices declined as foreign interests and even domestic institutions pulled out of the market, leaving it stagnant for the best part of a decade. Throughout this period France had an economic growth rate of some 6–7 per cent p.a. and many people have been unable to understand how the equity market could have remained at such low levels under these circumstances. The basic reason has been a lack of either institutional or domestic support and until this underlying position alters there is every reason for future buyers of French shares to be cautious, for unless domestic interest is increased and market mechanisms are improved by the planned reforms, a repeat of the Bourse's performance in the years after 1962 is always possible.

During the sixties several moves were made to stimulate the Bourse, notably the changes of the tax laws in 1965 which led to the abolition of withholding taxes on dividends paid to residents. The new regulations gave the shareholder a tax credit or avoir fiscal equal to 50 per cent of the value of dividends received. One of the results of the Baumgartner report is that this tax benefit has now been extended to certain non-residents, in an effort to make investment in French shares more attractive to foreigners.

The Commission also made several other major recommendations, as a result of which modifications are being made to facilitate rudimentary block trading. A system of jobbers or contrepartistes is also to be introduced and Agents de Change are to be allowed to create partnerships or firms as opposed to retaining full personal liability; they are also to be permitted to manage portfolios. These reforms affecting the mechanism of the market may eventually lead to a situation where trading will continue throughout lengthened market hours as in Britain today. It remains to be seen however whether enough of a priority has been given to increasing domestic interest in equities and contractual savings for France has one of the lowest ratios of shareholders of any country in Europe and their average age is the highest.

The French government is anxious to avoid having substantial amounts of the equity of French companies held outside France and is determined to ensure that the market is not swamped by the British. While wanting to improve the market for political reasons, the government hesitates directly to assist such a manifestation of capitalism. As a result, only those aspects of the Baumgartner report which improve market mechanisms and encourage foreign investment have so far been implemented. The government seems therefore to be partly bargaining on domestic interest in the equity market being revived by foreign interest, without them having to take any major measures to encourage a greater flow of savings into the private 'institutions' or stock market at the expense of the savings deposits they control. However, the French equity market will only be truly revitalised when it offers French investors better alternatives than they can find elsewhere.

The attention of French savers has to be drawn to the possible advantages of a thriving equity market, but on past results it will be difficult to put forward a totally convincing case. Undoubtedly, increased company information and the measures that have been taken will help, but an enormous amount will depend on whether the attitude of the authorities has in any way changed from that expressed in the French dictum repeated by Général de Gaulle: 'La politique de la France ne se fait pas à la Corbeille.'

Conclusion

France is a country which has a very high degree of central government control; economic objectives and policies are set out in five-year national plans and in order for the authorities to ensure that capital flows to the investments with the highest priority, they must control the financial market. We have seen how approximately 80 per cent of all medium- and long-term finance falls under potential government control, how the equity market lacks major sources of funds and how companies are dependent on government agencies for debt finance which they receive if their objectives coincide with those of the National Plan. Thus while Paris may offer many profitable opportunities to City operators, success will be hard to achieve unless they are prepared to adapt their methods and attitudes to those of the French. For one thing is certain, the French are extremely unlikely to modify their own systems merely to suit foreign intruders.

Chapter Five

The German Financial System

Unlike other countries in the Community, Germany until recently possessed not one, but several financial centres. This was a result partly of the allied dismemberment of the German banking system after the war, which put Dusseldorf, Hamburg and Frankfurt on an equal footing, and partly of the importance of the regional banks, most of which are owned by local municipalities or Länder. Despite these regional differences, the larger banks now operate throughout Germany and Frankfurt has clearly emerged as the most important financial centre.

In contrast with this geographical diversity, the German financial system is dominated by the banks, most of which now undertake the whole range of banking activities, but with differing degrees of emphasis. This state of affairs has led to their being labelled department store or all-purpose banks, and criticised for their substantial participations in industry and their stranglehold on the equity markets.

The Banking Institutions

Due to the similarity of function of so many different institutions German banking presents a confusing picture. The various types of bank can be divided as follows (see also table 11):

All-purpose banks:
- (a) The commercial banks: the Big Three, regional and other commercial banks, and private banks.
- (b) The savings banks and central Giro institutions.
- (c) The industrial and agricultural credit co-operatives and their central institutions.

Special banks:
- (d) The private and public mortgage banks.
- (e) Building and loan associations.

After the war the banks and financial markets had to start again from almost nothing and it was not therefore surprising that the fifties was marked by a gradual increase in long-term business. With the return of confidence, savers were prepared to commit their savings to longer-term investment and at the same time the banks were able to increase the proportion of medium- and long-term loans.

This change of emphasis from short- to long-term financing had its effects on the structure of the banking system. The mortgage banks and savings banks which concentrated on long-term finance benefited most. The commercial banks with almost 60 per cent of short-term business not surprisingly suffered a decline in their share of total savings as did the credit co-operatives.

During the sixties the banking institutions more than trebled their volume of business, but despite this impressive growth rate, which was considerably higher than the growth of GNP, the commercial banks could not match the rate of expansion of the building and loan associations and insurance companies. The three major categories of 'all-purpose banks' each increased their market share but by 1970 the savings banks had become the most powerful group in German banking accounting for two-fifths of banking business. Their success can be largely attributed to their extensive branch networks which enable them to tap the small saver and, to the advantages of being non-profit making, community-owned institutions. They also widened the range of services offered to bring themselves into direct competition with the commercial banks. The search for deposits was even further stimulated by the abolition of interest rate controls in 1967 and has resulted in an increase in the number of branches from 30,000 in 1960 to 48,000 in 1970, although the number of banks fell as a result of mergers.

Bank Involvement in Industry

To British eyes, one of the most remarkable aspects of the German banking system is its involvement in industry and in the securities markets.

The banks' own investments include major participations in many leading German companies. Although the Big Three are not the only banks to have taken such participations their activities in this field have attracted more attention than those of other banks. Banks are only obliged by law to declare equity interests of over 25 per cent and of non-financial holdings the Deutsche Bank owns 25 per cent or more of the equity of Daimler Benz; Karstadt, the department store chain; Sud-deutsche Zucker, the sugar company and Hapag Loyd, the biggest shipping company. The Dresdner Bank for its part has 25 per cent interests in twenty-one non-financial companies of which the largest is Metallgesellschaft (itself owning participations in other companies), Kaufhof, another large department store in which the Bayerische Hypotheken und Wechsel Bank also has a large interest and the Schultheiss Brauerei. These three companies alone accounted for approximately 40 per cent of the total equity holdings of the Dresdner Bank in 1970. The Commerzbank has fourteen interests of more than 25 per cent among which are the two department stores Karstadt and Kaufhof, various breweries and a hotel chain. Of the Big Three, the Deutsche and Dresdner banks have been the most active in this field during the past decade though none of these banks is pursuing what could be called aggressive policies. Indeed a youngish banker told us that the relationships between the older generation of bank and industry chiefs which had led to a number of these close ties, were now a thing of the past and that the younger generation of bankers was likely to change many of the old traditions.

Other banks and particularly the Westdeutsche Landesbank and the two Bavarian banks, the Bayerische Hypotheken and the Vereinsbank, have been somewhat more active. The Westdeutsche Landesbank has over 25 per cent interests in almost thirty outside concerns and according to a competitor is rapidly overtaking the Big Three.

Many people claim that over 60 per cent of German industry is now controlled by the banks, and while the statistics of direct ownership do not support this, the banks' power is undoubtedly very much greater than the figures suggest. In addition to its indirect holdings a bank, in its privileged position as company banker, often with board representation, has considerable unquantified influence on the affairs of the company. They also benefit from the use of bearer shares and the fact that most shares are deposited with them for safe custody and are held in blocks at the central Kassenverein, the equivalent of the French SICOVAM. Customers generally transfer voting rights to the banks but, contrary to what is generally assumed, the banks are by law required to ask the shareholders for voting instructions. Normally, the banks will circularise proxy voting details recommending certain action and asking for the customer's approval. The shareholder is, however, perfectly entitled to disagree with the bank and appear at the meeting himself, or if he feels strongly enough he can send in his own recommendations, which have by law to be circulated to all known shareholders. Nonetheless, despite the efforts of companies such as Volkswagen, the banks in practice appear to have almost unrestricted voting power, as shareholders who deposit their shares with the banks usually play a passive role, allowing the banks to represent and act for them at shareholders' meetings. This has meant that there are bank officers on the supervisory boards (Aufsichsrat) of companies in which the banks themselves have majority holdings and also on certain boards as the representatives of their customer shareholders.

There are of course advantages in close ties between banks and industry. Banks have been able to aid industries at critical periods by either taking over companies which run into difficulties or by buying shares from a major shareholder who wishes to dispose of his holding. A typical example was the Deutsche Bank's incursion into the rubber industry; family shareholdings were sold to the bank which then restructured the industry and finally sold off its participation. The Bavarian banks are at this moment involved in restructuring the brewing industry in southern Germany.

Herr Ulrich of the Deutsche Bank summarised the case for participations in a recent speech: 'When participations are for sale, where a company might be subject to unwelcome outside influence, in cases of financial reorganisation, estates settlement and so on, it is so often necessary to find a financially strong buyer or partner who can assist in finding a constructive solution. This is the proper role for the banks in that it offers them a business opportunity as well. Nevertheless the bank should not only acquire participations but should offer them for sale in due course as well. Between 1952 and 1970 the Deutsche Bank has sold thirty-one participations of more than 25 per cent; twenty-three of these were acquired during the same period.'

On the other hand there are substantial arguments against allowing banks to take participations in industry, such as the lender–shareholder conflict of interest which must arise where the banks have a major shareholding. Companies may also be restricted by the banks' unwillingness to grant finance for specific projects but it seems that there are very few companies which are so closely tied to a particular bank that they are unable to turn elsewhere for finance. Indeed the Big Three all maintain that increased competition in all aspects of banking business has meant that there are very few cases indeed where the banks have the power to dictate terms to an industrial company.

There remain strong political arguments against such a concentration of power in so few hands even if the banks are careful not to abuse their position. Indeed, it may be suggested that the Big Three have been reluctant to increase their participations as this would be certain to provoke counter-measures, although this is not so true for the other banks, which have been freer to adopt a more acquisitive policy. Banks in theory at least are only restricted by the level of their capital plus reserves, and one can argue that they are under an obligation to invest their funds in as profitable a way as possible. Although the question is complicated by the public ownership of some banks it is difficult to suggest what effective measures the government could in fact take to reduce the banks' power. Hiving off their industrial interests into holding companies on the Belgian pattern would have little practical effect although it would go some way to mute political criticism. The banks would naturally like to forestall any government action, and indeed the Deutsche Bank has already considered a voluntary hiving-off operation, but concluded that it was not at the moment viable for tax and legal reasons. Although the position is now quiet, it seems unlikely that the banks will be left in peace indefinitely.

Whether or not one is impressed by the banks' arguments in relation to their power over German industry no one can deny the banks' total domination of the equity market. Not merely do they own and issue shares and bonds, but also act as stockbrokers, manage unit trust funds and bond issues, and sell unit trusts and bonds to their customers through their branch network. The bulk of trading in shares is also undertaken by the banks, but whereas a short time ago it was estimated that at least 80 per cent of all share transactions were arranged by the banks and never reached the stock exchanges, the banks are now thought to be passing deals through the market, although they are still not required by law to do so.

The Commercial Banks

In 1971 there were 303 commercial banks in Germany with about 5,000 branches and 130,000 employees. These break down into: the big three banks (Deutsche Bank, Dresdner Bank, Commerzbank), regional and other commercial banks and private banks.

The commercial banks have always dominated the field of short-term lending of up to twelve months and recently they have accounted for an average of over 50 per cent of all short-term lending to companies. Since 1950, however, short-term business has been a decreasing proportion of their overall business as other services have been increased, particularly medium- and long-term lending which now accounts for almost a quarter of their total volume of business.

Such short-term loans are financed chiefly from sight, time and savings deposits but also from the rediscounting of bills of exchange through the Central Bank and from raising funds on the money market. However, the growth in time and savings deposits over the past twenty years in which the banks have managed to increase their share of business has enabled them to play a greater part in medium-term lending.

The long-term side of the business has been increased as a result of the commercial banks, and in particular the Big Three, taking an interest in the mortgage business and lending out of their own resources. While the commercial banks are not permitted to make mortgage loans directly, the Big Three have managed to some extent to circumvent this handicap by taking major participations in mortgage banks—for example the Dresdner Bank's majority holdings in Deutsche Hypothekenbank and Saechsische Bodencreditanstalt; the Deutsche Bank's majority holding in the Frankfurter Hypothekenbank and the Commerzbank's holding in the Westdeutsche Bodenkreditanstalt.

The Big Three are the largest privately owned banks in Germany. After the war they were split up into thirty institutions, each operating only in one federal 'Land', but in 1956 the components were reformed into the three banks, with central offices in Frankfurt and Dusseldorf and their operations, ranging from deposit to investment banking, spread throughout Germany. They are also very active internationally, especially in the Eurocurrency markets. Domestically they account for over 20 per cent of all short-term bank loans although they have a significantly lower proportion of medium- and long-term business.

The regional and other commercial banks differ from the Big Three in that they generally restrict themselves to a particular geographical area or industrial sector. As a result of the merger between the Bayerische Vereinsbank and the Bayerische Staatsbank in March 1971 the Vereinsbank is the largest regional commercial bank with assets of some DM 16 billion and 331 branches. The Bayerische Hypotheken und Wechselbank is close behind with assets of around DM 15 billion. These two banks have the advantage of being able to carry out a full range of mortgage business as well as general banking business. The next largest bank in this sector is the Bank für Gemeinwirtschaft which has 221 branches and is owned by local trade unions and co-operative societies.

In 1971 there were 159 private banks. These are generally run as sole proprietorships or partnerships and carry out a variety of investment banking functions and other financial services similar to those of the British merchant banks. Few of them possess more than a handful of branches—the Bankgeschäft Karl Schmidt being one of the major exceptions with eighty branches throughout Bavaria. Direct competition from the giant banks with freedom to operate in any profitable field they choose is however causing the private bankers a major problem and

63

most of them we talked to foresaw a large number of mergers over the next few years. Indeed one banker said, 'they will all have been eaten up unless they merge'. Burkhardt and Trinkaus have already heeded his warning and merged but as in England there is still a band of stalwarts who feel that there will always be room for small banks to 'prosper in the crevices between the mountainous ones'. Some banks like Bankhaus Gebrüder Bethman are opening branches in an effort to attract deposits although this must be an expensive operation. Others such as Georg Hauck und Sohn are active on the international front specialising in investment advice for foreign and domestic institutions.

The Savings Bank and Central Giro Institutions

These are now the largest group of financial institutions in Germany, accounting for over 38 per cent of all banking business. They are mostly owned by the local municipalities in which they operate and part of any surplus they make is distributed to the communities they serve.

Savings banks are of two distinct types; the 817 Sparkassen or regional savings banks with just over 15,000 branches and the twelve Central Giro Institutions or 'Girozentralen', which act as the regional clearing houses and reserve depositories. Formerly the Sparkassen were almost entirely involved in the collection of savings deposits, part of which they passed back to the public in the form of mortgage loans, and part of which was passed on to the central Girozentralen. The Girozentralen in turn are the major source of long-term funds for the local authorities and nationalised industries. However, the Sparkassen have never been compelled to take up the Girozentralens' bonds and indeed recently have found it more profitable to deal in the open market particularly with the insurance companies, thus making the Giros compete for their funds.

Apart from these traditional activities the savings banks and central Giro institutions have been taking on more and more regular banking activities over recent years and today offer the full range of commercial banking services. They control 42 per cent of all medium- and long-term finance which is generally channelled to housebuilding and local authorities. Other aspects of their business are hardly less impressive for they control almost 30 per cent of all short-term lending and hold 50 per cent of all banks' holdings of securities. The best-known central Giro is the Westdeutsche Landesbank formed by the merger of two central Giro institutions in 1968. It is now the largest financial institution in Germany with assets at the end of 1970 of DM 38.7 billion. Under aggressive management it has developed a full range of domestic banking services, is prominent in the international field and was one of the founding members of ORION.

The central institution of the savings bank sector is the Deutsche Girozentrale with assets of DM 12 billion; it administers a substantial volume of funds deposited by the central Giros and also grants loans to local authorities.

The Credit Co-operatives and their Central Institutions

The credit co-operatives and their central institutions have a smaller share of business than the commercial banks and savings banks but are nevertheless important in that they account for nearly 11 per cent of all bank lending. The credit co-operatives are divided into 686 industrial co-operatives known as Volksbanken and 6,300 agricultural co-operatives not all of which are active (one of the least active is the Bayerische Bauerkarottenkooperativ). Most of their business is in granting short- and medium-term loans to the farmers and tradesmen who form the bulk of their membership. As with the savings bank sector, their central institutions act as clearing houses and reserve depositories but they do not issue bonds and have made little impact as yet on the international front. However, this sector as a whole has become an important purchaser of domestic securities over recent years. Whether or not they will follow the Girozentralen into the international arena is an open question but it will be interesting to see whether they will be able to capitalise further on their wide deposit base. The Deutsche Genossenschaftskasse is at the centre of this sector which accounts for assets of over DM 27 billion.

The Private and Public Mortgage Banks

The mortgage banks are divided into twenty-nine private and seventeen public mortgage banks which grant long-term loans for housebuilding and other construction purposes. Whereas the private mortgage banks have increased their share of business over the past few years, the public mortgage banks have lost out mainly due to the diminishing importance of the government housing schemes which they operate. Both sets of institutions obtain most of their funds by means of selling mortgage bonds (Pfandbriefe) and other communal bonds which now account for one-third of all the bonds in circulation.

Building and Loan Associations

To quote the Bundesbank, 'The fifteen private and twelve public building and loan associations are collective organisations of persons wishing
to save for building purposes.' Since the war they have absorbed roughly
a quarter of all private savings each year and have provided over 30 per
cent of all the funds required to finance housebuilding. They are
popular with the public, not simply because their loans are a relatively
cheap and efficient method of financing housebuilding but also because
savings through these institutions attract government bonuses and tax
savings. It is this aspect more than any other which enables the building
and loan associations continually to attract such a large percentage of the
nation's savings. Indeed the Bundesbank states that the extent of this
assistance may make a savings contract for building purposes appear
rewarding even if there is no intention of taking up a loan. Government
assistance has therefore given the building and loan associations a considerably larger inflow of funds than they could otherwise expect.
However, recently the building and loan associations have been facing
increasing competition from the banks who are offering personal
mortgage loans and this has led them to devise more attractive forms
of loans themselves. Their future does, however, depend on whether
the government revises its present incentives for saving under this
scheme.

Savings Patterns and Company Finance

As elsewhere in Europe household saving is the most important source
of new finance and amounted to 28 per cent of total gross savings in
1970. Householders have a variety of choice as to where they place their
savings and to a certain extent can be cajoled to place their funds where
the government wants them. The best example of this has been government assistance for the housing sector which has since the war made
savings with building and loan associations an extremely favourable
investment. The volume of funds placed with insurance companies has
also increased due in part to recent government measures. However, as
one German banker said, 'Individual plans for the formation of wealth
generally follow the simple pattern of firstly placing funds in savings
deposits, then acquiring bonds and finally acquiring shares; the problem
is that there are few people with sufficient wealth to go so far as investing
in shares.' Recent studies by the Federal Government indicate that it
was the lower-income groups which were induced to save more by the
recent tax incentive measures and it seems likely that the great increase

Table 11: Balance Sheet Breakdown of German Banks in %

1970	Banking Group	ASSETS			LIABILITIES of which:		
		Vol. of Business	Loans to Non-Banks	Security Holdings	Sight Deps.	Savings Deps.	Bonds
Commercial Banks	Comm. Banks	25	23	24	40	16	7
	(Big Three)	(10)	(10)	(9)	(22)	(9)	(0)
Savings Banks	Savings Banks	38	38	52	37	60	38
	(Central Giros)	(15)	(15)	(14)	(4)	(0)	(38)
	(Savings Banks)	(23)	(23)	(37)	(33)	(60)	(0)
Credit Companies	Co-operative Banks	12	9	15	15	18	1
	(Central Co-ops)	(4)	(1)	(8)	(1)	(0)	(1)
	(Credit Co-ops)	(8)	(8)	(7)	(14)	(18)	(0)
Mortgage Banks	Mortgage Banks	14	20	2	0	0	45
	Private	(6)	(9)	(1)	(0)	(0)	(33)
	Public	(8)	(11)	(1)	(0)	(0)	(12)

Source: Monthly report of the Deutsche Bundesbank.

in the savings deposits with the banks in 1970 and 1971 was the result of this large body of new savers who followed the traditional pattern by placing their first savings with the banks. At the same time, only DM 8·5 billion was placed in the security markets in 1971 compared with the DM 11 billion in 1970, possibly a discouraging sign for the stock market but certainly an indication that this new group of savers are not familiar with securities. Private individuals have on average placed over 60 per cent of their savings with the banks over the past three years and approximately 50 per cent in savings deposits. Roughly 15 per cent of their savings have been used to purchase bonds and shares, leaving most of the transformation to be done by the banks (see table 12).

Table 12: Household Savings Patterns in Billions of DM

	1969	1970	1971
SAVINGS AND CAPITAL TRANSFERS	52	58	67
Invested in:			
Housing	10	12	14
Financial Assets	42	46	53
Of Which:			
Savings Deposits	21	21	28
Bank Savings Bonds	2	1	2
Funds with B & L Assoc.	4	5	5
Funds with Insurance Coys	7	8	10
Acquisition of Bonds	5	9	7
Acquisition of Shares	3	2	2
Currency and Sight Deposits	4	4	6
TOTAL	46	50	60
Less Liabilities			
Bank and other loans	(4)	(4)	(7)
FINANCIAL ASSETS ACQUIRED	42	46	53

Source: Monthly report of the Deutsche Bundesbank.

Sixty-four per cent of gross investment takes place in the industrial sector with the housing sector accounting for roughly 19 per cent and the public sector 15 per cent. As in France, the government has been able to finance its investments out of its own resources over the past three years, but housing and construction have required enormous volumes of finance, totalling over half of gross investment during the early sixties.

The enormous volume of funds which had to be channelled to reconstruction after the devastation of the war has had its effect on the way companies finance their investments. Unable to secure large volumes of funds externally, companies have had to rely substantially on retained earnings and depreciation, though over the past decade retained earnings have declined as a source of finance, largely as a result of rising costs and growing competition. The self-financing ratio has, however, remained at a high level in comparison with other countries and whereas it has averaged a steady 65 per cent over the past three years it was as high as 80 per cent in 1967 and 1968. The figures in table 13 also reveal the

Table 13: Company Financing in Billions of DM

	1967	1968	1969	1970	1971
Undistributed Profit	9	20·5	18·5	25	17
Capital Transfers	14	15	14	17	19
Depreciation	52·5	57	61	71	81
Internal Resources	75	92	93	113	117
Gross Investment	86	108	133	160	172
Own Resources	71	86	87	106	109
External Resources	15	22	46	54	63
Self-financing Ratio	82%	80%	66%	66%	64%

Source: Monthly report of the Deutsche Bundesbank.

gradual increase in depreciation as a source of finance due to the continued high rate of capital investment. Companies now, however, rely more on external financial resources and as with the housing sector their chief source of finance is the banks (see table 14). Another interesting feature in table 14 is the increase of bond and equity issues as a source of finance. Although this is still a relatively small proportion of the total external financial package, it is nevertheless a significant development from the stock market's point of view. Companies also made substantial use of the large inflow of foreign funds brought about by speculation on the revaluation of the Deutschmark in May 1971. At that time it was probably just as well that international monetary conditions enabled German companies to raise short- and medium-term finance abroad at favourable rates, as otherwise some companies may have found themselves in embarrassing positions having overcommitted themselves on long-term investment projects.

Table 14: External Sources of Company Finance

	1969	1970	1971
		Billions of DM	
External Finance Requirement	45	54	63
Acquisition of Financial Assets	20	25	29
TOTAL FINANCE REQUIRED	65	79	92
Financed by:			
Longer-term Bank Loans	28	30	40
Building & Loan Assoc. Loans	4	6	4·5
Insurance Company Loans	3	3	5
Sale of Bonds	0·5	1·5	4
Sale of Shares	3	3	5
Other Direct Loans	1·5	5·5	11
Shorter-term Bank Loans	20·5	12·5	16
Other Short-term Loans	4	17	8
	65	79	92

Source: Monthly report of the Deutsche Bundesbank.

Table 15: Assets of German Insurance Companies

	DM Billion	%
Mortgage loans	15·8	20
Loans against Borrowers' Notes	23·9	31
Securities	21·8	28
Participations	1·6	2
Real Estate	10·3	13
Equalisation Claims	3·6	5
Advance Payments	1·1	1
	78·1	100

Source: Monthly report of the Deutsche Bundesbank.

Institutional Investors

Although much less important than the banks as a direct source of long-term funds to companies, the insurance companies nevertheless play a significant role (tables 14 and 15). Despite not being permitted to have more than 20 per cent of their funds invested in equities insurance companies have fairly substantial participations in industrial companies. Allianz Versicherung of Munich, the largest insurance company, had in

1971 participations of more than 25 per cent in a number of important companies including 25 per cent of the Deutsche Continental-Gas Gesellschaft, 36 per cent of the Portland Cement Fabrik Hendjsen AG and 28 per cent of Schiess AG. Another insurance company Gerling Konzern of Cologne had in 1971 a 10 per cent stake in BMW. However, unlike the banks they generally do not take an active interest in the management of the companies in which they have participations.

Apart from the insurance companies, other sources of long-term capital are the social insurance funds and pension funds. The social insurance system has derived its resources from the excess of current receipts over benefit payments for the old age pension and unemployment insurance programmes. Up till 1966 they had managed to amass assets of DM 27 billion but since then deficits began to reduce total assets so that by mid-1969 holdings of securities had declined to a mere DM 7 billion. Most of their investments in securities takes the form of bank bonds, while their holdings of public authority securities and equities are negligible. However, as a result of recent problems new regulations have been introduced under which social insurance funds will not be allowed to invest any resources long-term unless their liquidity reserves have reached the prescribed level, and if longer-term investments are to be made, priority is to be given to social considerations.

Most pension funds in Germany are incorporated in the balance sheets of their own companies. There are now signs of change as the undesirability of this state of affairs is realised and already over forty pension funds supply long-term funds to the capital market. In June 1970 pension funds had assets of over DM 10 billion of which nearly DM 2 billion was invested in mortgage loans and DM 2·5 billion in securities. Needless to say the banks are the investment advisers to the pension funds which are officially supervised by the relevant Bundesaufsichtsamt in the same way as the insurance companies.

The other main category of institutional investors is the investment funds which were created by the banks to appeal especially to the smaller investors and in 1969 it was estimated that over 90 per cent of their sales were to private individuals. The management companies are in fact owned and controlled by groups of banks although they operate through separate companies. The Dresdner Bank is an exception to this rule in that it owns its own investment fund entirely. Although they are called investment funds, giving the impression of a closed-end British investment trust, they are in fact open-ended and follow the same principle as unit trusts in that the price of the units is determined by the overall value of the fund.

After a somewhat disappointing period during the early sixties, when new subscriptions to the investment funds gradually declined, the position began to pick up from the mid-sixties, probably due in part to the activity of American mutual funds, particularly IOS, which caused German bankers to realise the potential for this form of saving. There was also an added incentive in that the funds provided an excellent opportunity for the banks to rid themselves of the multitude of small equity investors who, having to deal entirely through the banks, involved them in considerable paperwork. Whereas in 1960 a mere DM 340 million was invested in investment funds, by 1969 the German public had purchased more than DM 5 billions' worth of mutual fund units and a further DM 2·1 billions' worth of foreign mutual fund units. Sales of domestic and foreign investment fund certificates had by 1965 reached some 7 per cent of household long-term savings as against the 1 per cent in 1963 and by 1969 the figure had rocketed to some 19 per cent. However, the mutual funds suffered a severe setback in 1970 as a result of the IOS crisis. 'The Nightmare of IOS', as one banker put it, is now over and mutual funds are responsible for over 30 per cent of all trading on the German equity market.

In 1971 there were fifteen investment companies managing fifty-five mutual funds with total net assets of DM 11 billion compared with 1964 when there were only ten mutual fund companies managing twenty-four equity funds. Although the majority of the funds today are based on the domestic equities of German companies, some offer 'a cocktail of mixed risk' and others specialise in fixed interest securities and foreign securities. Recently, five property funds have been established which have done particularly well. Of the DM 5·5 billion which were invested in funds in 1969, roughly half went to equity funds and half to bond funds. Bond funds have also been successful because they offer a greater degree of security than equity funds and generally guarantee a relatively higher yield, reflecting the staid approach of the German investor. The future development of investment funds lies with the banks. It is they which sell the units through their branches and it is up to the individual branch manager of a particular bank to advise his customers. Bank managers' performance used to be judged by the volume of savings accounts, thus providing little incentive to recommend the purchase of equities or units, but this attitude is reported to be changing. Whether to the banks' advantage or not it does now seem that there is a growing preference amongst private individuals for saving through these units.

Closed-end funds have been virtually prohibited in Germany as indeed have funds holding certificates of other investment fund units.

As a result of the IOS fiasco the laws regarding foreign investment funds have been considerably tightened up and the new conditions are approximately the same now for both domestic and foreign investment fund companies.

The Bond Market

The structure of the bond market has changed over the past ten years in that of the three types of bank bonds, communal bonds—many of which are issued by the Girozentralen and taken up by the savings banks—have now outstripped mortgage bonds not merely in new issues but also in circulation. The funds raised by the issue of communal bonds, however, do not merely provide finance in the form of loans for the municipalities but also for the State and increasingly for industry and housebuilding, although mortgage bonds are still the chief source of finance for building purposes. The public authorities have the next largest volume of bonds in circulation, DM 32·5 billion in 1970 of which the Bundesbahn—the Federal Railway—accounted for DM 7 billion and the Post Office for a further DM 5 billion. During the mid-sixties considerable strain was placed on the bond market by the imposition of a 25 per cent capital yield tax on the interest earned on German bonds held by non-residents—a move designed to stave off the large in-flow of capital from abroad. The ruling although perhaps beneficial to the economy had far-reaching consequences for the bond market and in particular for industrial bonds. Foreigners sold domestic bonds and transferred the proceeds to foreign bonds which were not subject to this tax, and as a consequence industrial bonds and public authority bonds, of which over 40 per cent had been subscribed by non-residents, were badly hit. Industrial bonds have never really recovered and industry has largely turned its back on the bond market as a source of long-term finance; industrial bonds in circulation at the end of 1971 amounted to a mere DM 9 billion (see table 16) and it is only a few large companies which have sufficient stature to tap the market.

Industry has come to rely almost entirely on the banks for the remainder of its medium- and long-term credit needs. A certain proportion of the credits extended from the banks are in the form of indirect bond financing, as the banks merely pass on credit to industry which they in turn finance by issuing bonds on the market. Apart from medium- and long-term credit, the banks supply funds to industry through 'Schuldscheindarlehen', or loans against borrowers' notes. This form of finance arose chiefly because the 2·5 per cent tax on new security issues applied only to industrial and foreign borrowers. The loans against

Table 16: Total Bonds in Circulation in Billions of DM

	End 1960	End 1970
Public Authority Bonds	6·92	32·50
Mortgage Bonds	14·95	48·37
Communal Bonds	9·91	50·79
Other Bank Bonds	3·49	18·65
Industrial Bonds	5·13	7·74
TOTAL	40·41	158·00

Source: Monthly report of the Deutsche Bundesbank.

borrowers' notes are similar to bonds but are handled outside the securities market thus avoiding the discriminatory tax. They are attractive to investors in that they generally carry a slightly higher rate of interest than ordinary bonds and yet the cost to the companies is less not merely due to the tax advantages but also because there are no advertising or printing expenses. Although the banks grant most of these loans, they assign a large percentage to institutional investors such as the insurance companies. At the end of 1966 the volume of these notes had not quite reached DM 10 million but by the end of 1970 this figure had more than doubled and now represents a substantial form of long-term finance for industry.

The Equity Market

Table 17 reveals that equity has been an increasing source of long-term finance for industrial companies, though it still forms a relatively small proportion of total external finance raised. Companies are however sometimes under pressure to raise equity if only to satisfy the debt–equity ratios required by law for life assurance companies to invest in their shares and this can result in rights issues at unfavourable moments. At the end of 1970 there were roughly 2,500 registered AG (Aktien Gesellschaft) companies of which only 552 were quoted on the stock exchanges. The number of quoted companies, however, was greater in 1966 (605) than 1971 (550); the reduction has been brought about to some extent by companies changing from the AG to GmbH (Gesellschaft mit beschrankter Haftung) status to avoid certain legal requirements such as disclosure. Since 1965 over eighty companies have disappeared from the Stock Exchange and only eleven new companies have sought quotations.

There are eight Stock Exchanges in Germany of which the most important are situated in Frankfurt and Dusseldorf. Most opinion we

Table 17: Sales of Securities in Millions of DM

	1969	1970	1971
FIXED INTEREST SECS			
1. Net Sales of Domestic Bonds*	12,382	14,312	20,579
Bank Bonds	12,258	11,935	14,857
of which:			
Mortgage Bonds	3,145	1,901	4,369
Communal Bonds	7,265	7,652	7,122
Other Bank Bonds	1,849	2,382	3,366
Public Authority Bonds	288	2,158	4,280
Industrial Bonds	−164	220	1,442
2. Net Acquisition of Foreign Bonds	5,365	1,042	−1,182
TOTAL CAPITAL RAISED (1+2)	17,747	15,354	19,397
SHARES			
1. Sales of Domestic Shares (Market Value)	2,797	3,591	4,736
2. Net Acquisition of Foreign Shares by Residents	5,627	2,669	1,872
TOTAL CAPITAL RAISED IN			
EQUITY MARKET (1+2)	8,424	6,260	6,608

* Gross sales at market value less redemptions.

Source: Monthly report of the Deutsche Bundesbank.

heard indicated that there is little chance of a centralised Stock Exchange in the next few years, though the volume of the transactions in Bremen, Hanover and Stuttgart is low. German equity market capitalisation is over £13 billion. As indicated earlier it is the banks which dominate the market for they are the only members of the Stock Exchange—if you want to broke in Germany you have to bank as well. Foreign banks, which are subject to national banking laws, have been unable to carry out broking activities but the American firm 'Bache' became a member of the German stock exchange by buying a dormant bank. Private individuals or 'Freie Makler' are allowed to become members in order to deal on their own account but they cannot deal on behalf of the general public. There are no jobbers and during official market hours—11.30 a.m. to 1.30 p.m.—designated brokers fix the price at which the greatest number of orders can be matched; a considerable volume of business, however, takes place outside the official market.

The development of the equity market will in the long run depend on the attitudes and policies of the banks, for it is they which are in direct contact with the vast majority of the saving population. The chief criticism which can be levelled at the banks in this context is that bankers make most of their profits out of making loans and it is therefore not particularly in their interest to promote equity finance. Indeed one eminent banker told us that the 'banks are more interested in and have more expertise in bond and loan issues and so long as the banks remain the most important financial influence in Germany, the bond market will remain more important than the equity market . A more clear-cut statement would be difficult to find and the same banker went on to support his argument by saying that, 'for the saver it is difficult to improve on a return of 8 per cent while for the company, not merely are there fewer problems in that they only have a bank to deal with rather than a multitude of small investors, but the average company also prefers to pay interest on loans and bonds which is deductible for tax purposes rather than pay dividends'—an argument that will find little support in the City.

It has been estimated that between 50 and 60 per cent of the equity of the largest 150 German companies is in a very few hands—mostly the banks and insurance companies. In itself this is not disastrous for the equity market, but the real problem is that these holdings are permanent in nature and substantially restrict the market in shares. In addition it is the banks which are indirectly responsible for managing the unit trusts, which account for a further 10 per cent of equity market capitalisation. There have been other major factors which have affected the development of equity finance in Germany. Memories of the losses of the thirties, the lack of detailed financial information and experiences of IOS have all been major influences on the saver, whilst for the companies, so long as they can obtain as much loan finance as they need from the banks, there seems little reason why they should want to obtain more equity finance. It is also worth pointing out that German managers are not financially orientated, and corporate objectives tend to be defined in terms of sales and market penetration rather than earnings per share. The result of all these influences is an equity market that is narrow, underdeveloped and largely controlled by the banks. There is little indication, at the moment, that this situation will improve without considerable changes in the established structure of the German capital market.

Table 18: The Ownership of Securities in Millions of DM

(Nominal value unless otherwise stated)

	SHARES		FIXED INTEREST		INVESTMENT FUNDS†	
	1969	1970	1969	1970	1969	1970
Banks*	7,176‡	8,292	72,568	75,663	322	450
Private Individuals	11,720	12,052	26,396	31,779	5,560	6,495
Insurance Companies	1,075	1,182	14,634	16,055	232	286
Investment Funds	1,010	1,043	2,477	3,432	—	—
Business Enterprises	7,320	7,443	6,987	6,555	172	183
Social Soc. Funds	10	2	7,388	7,441	1	3
Other Public Assocns.	3,788	3,950	3,242	3,095	17	16
Foreign	2,623	2,845	2,707	4,199	398	455

Notes:
* Including the Deutsche Bundesbank and the Building and Loan Association.
† Investment Fund Units at Asset Value calculated by multiplying the number of units reported by the average value of one unit as at end 1970.
‡ Domestic Bank's holdings of shares and investment fund units at balance sheet value.

Source: Monthly report of the Deutsche Bundesbank.

Conclusion

The banks have a stranglehold on the German financial system. They control the equity and bond markets, 60 per cent of household savings pass through their hands, and they hold important participations in German industry. One can argue that competition is now extremely fierce both between individual banks and between the various classes of bank, and many banks are in fact publicly owned. Some cynics even suggest that the bureaucratic nature of German banking prohibits abuse of their potential power, as communications within banks, let alone between banks, are poor.

Nonetheless there is considerable cause for concern. The threat of government intervention is always present, but it is difficult to see what effective action could be taken, and even more difficult to see how a liberal financial climate could ever be established in Germany.

Chapter Six

The Dutch Financial System

Many people in Britain feel a much closer affinity to the Netherlands than to other member states of the Community. This is not only because of the marvellous Dutch facility for languages, which has made direct contact so easy, but also because many of their traditions and institutions have similarities to our own. This flows through to the commercial and financial world, with the result that the structure of its capital market is closer to ours than those of other members of the Community. In fact when London was developing its own financial markets, it copied some of the methods used in Amsterdam.

Up to the Napoleonic Wars, Amsterdam could claim to be the most important financial centre in the world, a position founded on Holland's skill as a trading nation. The Amsterdam merchant-bankers involved with the financing of international trade and the issue of Dutch foreign loans are also credited with having invented stock trading. In 1602 the Dutch East India Company was founded and was the first company in the world to issue shares by public offer. These shares were also the first to be traded on a public exchange and the success of this venture encouraged the extension of such activity, which resulted in a flourishing Stock Exchange. From 1850 onwards Amsterdam played a significant part in the financing of railways in the United States and in the early part of this century it was the most important market for American securities outside the United States. The proportion of foreign stocks quoted on the Amsterdam Bourse is still high, and Dutch bankers are active in the arbitrage markets.

Around this base a wide variety of institutions has grown up to channel long-term savings into investment: these include insurance and life assurance companies, pension funds and investment trusts all of which have wide investment powers. The contractual element in the pattern of savings is high, which again invites comparisons with the British system and which caused the Segré Report to take the Dutch capital market as a model for the rest of Europe.

In view of the similarities in approach and the fact that Holland is well placed to serve as a first base for British expansion into Europe, it is quite natural that many British companies have turned their attention to Holland. It is perhaps surprising to hear that some of these companies have had serious misgivings about the overall climate for investors, misgivings which are partly shared by a number of people in the Dutch financial community.

It is said that labour, represented by the unions, is too strong a force within the economy. As a result labour costs have escalated and profit margins have been eroded. This process is clearly illustrated in the graph. Equity investment is therefore becoming less attractive and this is borne out by the diminishing amounts of equity issues during the past five years. Correspondingly the ratio of own capital to borrowed capital has declined steadily since 1965 (table 19). This situation has led a number of commentators to state that Holland has reached a critical period and that strong action must be taken soon to improve the financial position of Dutch companies.

On the side of the investor the trend can be discerned by the unexciting performance of the Amsterdam Bourse until the beginning of 1972. It is interesting to note that much of the rise since has been due to British buying, and a number of Amsterdam bankers thought it likely that City investment managers had not done their homework properly and did not fully appreciate the underlying problems of the investor in Holland. Large Dutch financial institutions have been disinvesting out

Table 19: Relation of Own Capital to Borrowed Capital (in Millions of Guilders)

	Own Capital	Borrowed Capital
1965	30·627	15·956
1966	31·745	17·706
1967	33·276	21·571
1968	33·441	23·421
1969	37·497	29·724

	In percentages
1965	1·91
1966	1·79
1967	1·54
1968	1·47
1969	1·26

Source: Nederlandse Credietbank NV Annual Report 1970.

of Dutch shares in the past few years. For example one large financial institution had 75 per cent of its equity portfolio invested in Holland in 1960, while the proportion now is only 45 per cent.

WAGES AND NET PROFITS AS PERCENTAGE OF COMPANIES' TURNOVER

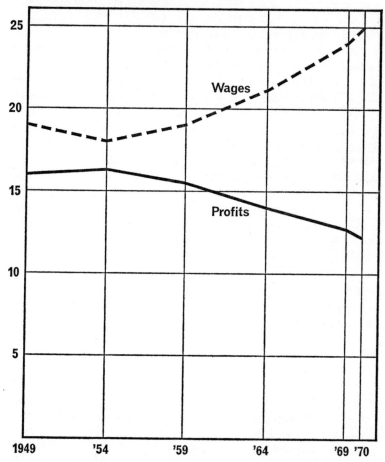

Source: Nederlands Credietbank NV, Annual Report 1970.

The advent of the Common Market gave rise to a process of concentration in industry which put some of the smaller Dutch manufacturing companies at a comparative disadvantage and this may have forced investment managers to look elsewhere.

Evidence of a more socially aware approach in Holland can be seen in other areas. For example taxation and social insurance contributions rose from 40·5 per cent of net national income in 1967 to 45 per cent in 1971. The Central Bank has played a more active—some would say too restrictive—role in recent years. Although in the past it has exerted its influence by unofficial means, like the Bank of England, its position may be strengthened by a Bill which has been before Parliament since 1970 and which has been the subject of considerable debate between the Central Bank and the banking community.

The most direct evidence of the problems of the labour situation in Holland which will have to be faced by any British company intending to expand in Holland, is the takeover code introduced in 1971. The first part is concerned with the code of practice to be followed in a takeover or merger and covers in particular the immediate disclosure of the existence of a bid situation, the intentions of the bidder, profit and asset figures and other matters such as inside dealings. The second part is entitled 'Rules of Conduct for the Protection of the Employees', and covers situations where more than a hundred employees are involved. It stipulates that the trade unions concerned must be informed of the bid before a public announcement is made and that the board shall inform the trade unions of the reasons which have led them to contemplate a merger and its expected economic and social consequences. The board must also be prepared to discuss in some detail with the unions the information which is supplied. From the document it is not clear what happens if the unions disagree, but the merger discussions have to be reported to the Minister of Economic Affairs who, no doubt, would have some say in the matter. It is interesting to note, however, that the code does not cover the protection of minority shareholders and it is still not unknown for victim companies to defend themselves by cancelling the voting rights outstanding and issuing new voting stock to supporters.

It would be easy to exaggerate the significance of some of the figures that have been presented so far, particularly as the Dutch economy is dominated by five big multi-national companies (Royal Dutch, Unilever, Philips, AKZO and Hoogevens, now merged with Hoescht). Nevertheless the mood in Dutch financial circles is one of uncertainty about the labour situation, which is implied by the comment: 'In Germany, the power of the banks counterbalances the power of the unions; in the Netherlands there is no such balance, and if the banks were to try to improve their position, they would find that they have left it too late, because the unions would not let them.' Another took a more philosophical view of the Dutch approach to commercial life: 'The trouble with Holland is that when you have a hole, you fill it in, and when you have a mountain, you flatten it.' This typifies the staid middle-class attitude and is the price that Holland has paid—if that is the right term—for its relative peace and prosperity during the past few centuries. Whether this approach will serve Holland well in the more competitive environment of the Community, or more particularly whether it will allow sufficient dynamism amongst the financial institutions to capitalise on the financial markets' relative strength and experience, is entirely another matter.

Savings Patterns

The rate of savings has traditionally been satisfactory and has amounted to just over 21 per cent of net national income during the past three years (table 20). By far the largest proportion of savings from households is done through the medium of life assurance and pension funds, the latter being funded, which is an unusual practice in the Community. The other important institutions which collect savings are the local savings banks, the farmers' co-operative banks, the post office savings bank, and the commercial banks. Table 21 shows that the life assurance companies and pension funds collected over 6 billion guilders in 1970 against the 2·7 billion guilders accounted for by the other groups combined. Of the group of savings banks, agricultural savings banks (or

Table 20: National Savings as a Percentage of Net National Income

	Average					
1959/60	1961/63	1964/55	1966/67	1968	1969	1970
21·8	19·0	19·7	19·1	21·2	21·5	21·1

Source: The Netherlands Bank Report for the year 1970.

Table 21: Net Supply of Funds from Institutional Investors on the Capital Market (in Billions of Guilders)

	1960	1965	1970
Life Assurance Companies and Pension Funds	1,731	3,109	5,681
Social Insurance Funds	168	90	−94
Savings Banks	1,090	1,819	2,884
	2,989	5,018	8,471

Source: The Netherlands Bank Report for the year 1970.

co-operative farmers' banks) are by far the most important, as can be seen in table 22. They have been attracting an increasing proportion of savings and now have about 45 per cent of total savings accounts. This growth reflects the prosperity of the agricultural community, their greater thrift and the strength of the agricultural banks' branch networks as new industries spread into rural areas and villages become suburbs. The figures also show that the commercial banks have also made considerable strides in this field since 1958.

Table 22: Total Balance on Savings Accounts (in Millions of Guilders)

	1951	1958	1964	1970
Post Office Savings Banks	1,298	2,142	3,880	5,999
General Savings Banks	1,236	2,329	4,857	8,753
Agricultural Credit Institutions	1,587	3,208	7,254	14,862
Total Savings Banks	4,121	7,679	15,991	29,614
Commercial Banks	50	322	2,043	5,332

Source: The Netherlands Bank Report for the year 1970.

Where investment in securities is concerned, the average Dutchman has a strong traditional preference for bonds. Yields are of much greater interest, even at a time of considerable inflation, than the possible capital growth of an equity investment, despite there being no capital gains tax. The Dutch are not by nature a nation of gamblers and the performance of the Amsterdam Stock Exchange up to the beginning of this year has confirmed many of their latent fears.

Banking Structure and Recent Developments

There have been considerable changes on the Dutch banking scene during the past few years and the stage is now set for a period of fairly intense competition. The largest bank in terms of deposits is the Co-operative Raiffeisen-Boerenleenbank which is the result of a recent merger of the two organisations of farmers' co-operative banks. At the end of 1971 it had a balance sheet total of 23·5 billion guilders, compared with Algemene Bank Nederland and Amsterdam-Rotterdam Bank (AMRO), which are the two other largest banks, with 22·2 and 19·8 billion guilders respectively. A list of the other principal banks can be seen in table 23.

The activities of the farmers' co-operative banks were traditionally to take deposits from and make credits and longer-term funds available to

Table 23: The Twelve Principal Dutch Banks

End 1971 (in Million Guilders)

	Balance Sheet Totals	Savings Deposits	Other Deposits	Profits before Tax
Co-op Raiffeisen-Boerenleenbank	23,525	16,980	1,433	69
Algemene Bank Nederland (ABN)	22,261	2,858	17,867	138
Amsterdam-Rotterdam Bank (AMRO)	19,808	2,703	15,505	140
Nederlandse Middenstandsbank*	7,639	1,779	5,297	55
Mees & Hope	3,341	3,068		27
Nederland Credietbank	2,625	2,467		20
Slavensburg's Bank	1,703	1,552		24
Van Lanschot (Mar. 1971)	1,503	1,463		na
Pierson, Heldring & Pierson (end 1970)	1,081	1,025		na
Banque de Paris et des Pays Bas	929	872		9
H. Albert de Bary & Co. (Sept. 1971).	915	881		19
Kas Associate	748	687		4

* 33 per cent Dutch government participation.

Source: The Banker, July 1972.

the farming community. However, they are now moving into direct competition with the commercial banks and have found their large deposit base and branch network in the rural areas a strong foundation on which to build. The commercial banks have also been subjected to competition from the postal giro system whose success a few years ago came as a surprise to the banking community. They set up their own giro system but the competition from the postal giro continues to be a problem. In 1970 most of the commercial banks had to increase the interest rate allowed on current account deposits, because the postal giro announced its intention to pay interest. After consultation with the government a rate of 2·5 per cent, calculated on the lowest balance for every half-month, was agreed, albeit reluctantly.

The commercial banks have responded by extending their branch networks and by competing for savings accounts. At the end of 1970 Algemene Bank had 572 branches, forty-four of which had been opened in the previous twelve months and in doing so have taken on the savings banks in the small towns and suburbs which serve the local tradesmen. Other banks like Mees & Hope have opened branches on a more selective basis, in order to provide a better service for their larger customers. Another counter to the threat from the savings and farmers' banks has been to join up with them, as Mees & Hope has done with the Nederlandse Spaarbankfond, in conjunction with the Westdeutsche Landesbank Girozentrale. The commercial banks, however, remain by far the strongest in foreign trade and securities. Most of their lending is naturally short-term, but in recent years they have increased their medium-term lending up to five years, which has been financed to a large extent by their savings accounts. They are precluded from taking more than 5 per cent of the equity of industrial or commercial companies, but have diversified their financial activities into hire-purchase, mortgage lending, leasing, factoring and even into package tours and the development of shopping centres. On the securities front they act as stockbrokers and managers and underwriters of new issues. As will be seen the most important part of the corporate new issue market for loans is private placements and a bank often acts as the intermediary. Most banks also run unit trusts in which their smaller clients are encouraged to invest, although this is sometimes done on a co-operative basis such as the Amro-Pierson Fund.

Other recent developments on the Dutch banking scene have included national mergers and participations by foreign banks. Both can be regarded as responses to the ever-increasing need for size in order to serve the needs of the expanding national and international corporations, and are part of the search for the greatest possible administrative efficiency. The AMRO Bank is the result of a merger between the Amsterdam and Rotterdam banks in 1964, while the Nederlansche Handel-Maatschappis De Twentsche Bank merged to form the Algemene Bank Nederland also in 1964, which itself took over the Hollandshe Bank-Unie in 1968. Morgan Guaranty has a 20 per cent interest in Bank Mees & Hope (which is again the result of a recent merger), Chase Manhattan 25 per cent of Nederlandsche Credietbank, and First National Bank of Chicago 20 per cent of Slavenburg's Bank.

Of the foreign banks operating in Holland the most important is Banque de Paris et des Pays Bas, which is almost regarded as a native bank. A number of American banks have opened branches in recent years, but First National City Bank can claim the distinction of having closed down two of its four branches (in Amsterdam and The Hague), much to the quiet satisfaction of the local banking community; it is quite possible however that this is misplaced and First National has other more effective plans up its sleeve. British banks are represented by

Lloyds & Bolsa International and Barclays International but their profits
have remained generally low and they do not seem to have made much
impact on the domestic scene.

Naturally the commercial banks have links with their industrial
customers and bankers are often appointed to the board of industrial
and commercial companies. The practice has become so widespread

Table 24: Supply and Demand on the Capital Market in 1970 (in Millions of Guilders)

1. *Net Domestic Supply*

Savings Banks	2,890
Life Assurance Companies, Pension Funds and Social Insurance Funds	5,610
Money-creating institutions	330
Personal and business sector	1,230
TOTAL	10,060
of which:	
Bonds and mortgage bank loans	1,030
Shares	950
Private and mortgage loans*	8,080

2. *Net Domestic Demand*

Public Sector	3,550
Private Sector	6,800
Money-creating institutions	430
TOTAL	10,780
of which:	
Bonds and mortgage bank bonds	2,480
Shares	210
Private and mortgage loans*	8,090

* Including property investments by institutional investors.

Source: The Netherlands Bank Report for the year 1970.

that the directorships of certain prominent bankers run into hundreds
and this has caused considerable criticism within Holland in the past
year, particularly from left-wing groups. They claim that bankers have
too much influence and it should be curbed. Bankers reply that these
directorships are purely of a supervisory nature and that they very
rarely become involved with management problems.

In order to increase their services, commercial banks have recently established corporate finance departments which are gradually building up the business of merger and takeover advice on a national and international scale. The banks' slowness in capitalising on their wide industrial and commercial contacts by not providing earlier this type of service has laid them open to criticism. But in their defence it should be mentioned that Dutch companies traditionally have not paid fees to banks for special services, and they are expected to meet these additional expenses out of their normal banking revenue.

Supply and Demand for Capital

The generally low level of new equity issues and the high proportion of government and local authority borrowing by public issues can be seen in tables 24, 25 and 26. A major reason in recent years has been the relatively poor performance of the stock market, in turn a result of declining profit margins on the part of companies which, it can be argued, find equity more expensive than debt finance. Private placements as a medium for borrowing are particularly important; these require comparatively few formalities as compared with public loans and are popular because issuing expenses are low (although the interest to be paid is somewhat higher). In addition terms and conditions can easily be tailored to suit individual borrowers' particular requirements. The arrangements are made by the banks and the loans, for fifteen to twenty-five years, are placed with institutions. Another reason for the lack of interest in equities is that the institutions have been increasing their interests in property.

Local authorities are pre-eminent in the organisation of non-private sector financing. The Bank for Netherlands Municipalities acts as the central institution covering public and private issues on behalf of local authorities. In addition there is a certain amount of local financing, whereby a local hospital, for example, can raise money from the community at favourable rates. The government is not directly involved but Central Bank authority is required for issues of more than 10 million guilders in order that the equilibrium of the market is maintained and is not overloaded. It is estimated that 50 per cent of public issues are taken up by individuals, a little less by insurance companies, pension funds and savings banks, and the rest by overseas investors. Compared with other Community countries, government institutions providing long-term finance to industry play a relatively minor role. The principal institutions are firstly the National Investment Bank in which the commercial banks have a minority participation, which makes medium- and

Table 25: Domestic Supply and Demand on the Capital Market (in Millions of Guilders)

Net Supply	1961	1966	1970
Institutional Investors	3,675	5,559	8,471
Shares	89	493	361
Bonds, including mortgage bank bonds	582	− 1	347
Private loans	2,026	3,411	4,632
Mortgage loans	769	1,160	2,345
Real property	209	496	786
Personal and business sector	134	1,043	1,107
Shares			593
Bonds, including mortgage bank bonds	88	1,013	713
Private loans	—	—	− 194
Mortgage loans	46	30	− 5
Money-creating institutions	561	177	479
Shares	94	14	− 8
Bonds, including mortgage bank bonds	174	− 39	− 26
Private loans	293	202	513
TOTAL	4,370	6,779	10,780

Net Demand			
Government	680	1,065	1,893
Bonds Issued	264	− 15	679
Private loans	416	1,080	1,214
Local Authorities	970	1,072	1,658
Bonds Issued	176	659	632
Private Loans	794	413	1,026
Private Sector	2,345	4,872	6,800
Shares	197	138	172
Bonds, including mortgage bank bonds	124	893	779
Private loans	1,000	2,149	2,708
Mortgage loans	815	1,196	2,355
Real Property	209	496	786
Money-creating institutions	60	82	429
Shares	60	1	38
Bonds, including mortgage bank bonds	—	81	391
TOTAL	4,055	7,091	10,780

Source: The Netherlands Bank Report for the year 1970.

Table 26: Public New Issues, Million Guilders

	Total					of which shares				
	1958	1963	1968	1969	1970	1958	1963	1968	1969	1970
Government Bank for Netherlands	245	996	728	1,319	1,090	—	—	—	—	—
Municipalities	706	497	937	820	829	—	—	—	—	—
Banks and Credit Institutions	158	17	66	208	489	1·6	8·1	9·6	24·9	10·4
Others	1,008	155	646	405	629	897·4	65·2	138·3	160·4	31·6
TOTAL	2,117	1,665	2,377	2,752	3,037	899·0	73·3	147·9	185·2	42·0

Source: Dutch Central Bureau of Statistics, 1971.

long-term credits available to the business sector and secondly the Netherlands Participation Bank which provides equity finance mainly for small and medium-sized companies which do not have ready access to the public capital market.

Insurance Companies and Pension Funds

It has already been made clear that such institutions play an important role in the supply of long-term capital to the market. Compared with similar institutions in the Community countries, the managers have wide investment powers though both insurance companies and pension funds are subject to the regulations of an Insurance Chamber. The split between the various types of investment of life assurance companies and pension funds varies as can be seen below.* There has however been considerable disinvestment out of Dutch equities in the last decade as has already been noted, while reinsurance companies, which have a greater requirement for quicker liquidation of their investments, tend to have slightly over 50 per cent in bonds and the rest in equities. Of the foreign investments of the institutional investors American shares are the most important accounting for approximately 30 per cent of the equity portfolios; Germany and Japan account for 10 per cent and a further 10 per cent is spread throughout the rest of Europe with little invested in Britain. Dutch institutional investors have had little faith in investment in Britain for some time and usually give devaluation fears and labour troubles as the reasons.

Like their British counterparts, institutional managers are not at all willing to become involved with the management of industrial or commercial companies where results have recently been disappointing. They have tended to use their main sanction which is to sell and this is perhaps one reason why they have welcomed the sudden interest of British institutions which have provided sufficient buoyancy in the market to enable them to do so. The banks fulfil an intermediary function in the provision of private loans and the larger loans are syndicated, which again does not encourage closer links between 'institutions' and industry.

* Portfolios of:

	1970		1969	
	Life Assurance Companies		*Pension Funds*	
Property	9%		13%	
Mortgages	21%		8%	
Securities	8%		40%	
Private Loans	41%		33%	
Other Investments	15%		6%	

Source: Dutch Central Bureau of Statistics.

Investment Trusts and Unit Trusts

Although unit trusts and investment trusts are not numerous in Holland, the Robeco group, which also manages Rolinco and Utilico, has considerable funds under its charge and has a wide international reputation. Robeco was an investment club formed in Rotterdam in 1929 by a number of businessmen who clubbed together to make money. In 1933 they had 1 million guilders and are now worth more than 3 billion guilders. Although the funds are in theory closed, the company buys and sells its own shares at a small commission. Other trusts have not performed so well and some found themselves in difficulties, which enabled Robeco to take them over at a discount. In order to broaden its base even further, Robeco has recently arranged for purchases and redemptions to be transmitted via the post giro service thus bringing its units within the reach of the small saver.

The Stock Market

The Stock Exchange has two categories of membership, individual and corporate. Corporations, including banks, are eligible provided their managing directors are individual members, who in turn are either brokers or specialists. The former act on behalf of clients, advising them and executing their orders. At the Stock Exchange the brokers as a rule call on the services of the specialists, called hoekmen, whose function is to collect buying and selling orders and match them as satisfactorily as possible. They are similar to stockjobbers in that they can only be approached by other members of the exchange and they are allowed to take positions under certain conditions in the stocks in which they specialise. If the hoekman cannot cope with the number of orders other brokers can deal amongst themselves in so-called 'open corners'. For most stocks two prices are struck each day, but there is continuous trading in international companies and other particularly active stocks. Banks are forced to put their orders through the Exchange and bargains are always made for cash. Although there are four hundred quoted companies, one experienced investment manager commented that the Dutch market in fact consists of the five international companies, about a further twenty blue chips and 100–150 medium- to small-sized companies with low P/Es and small marketability. It was not therefore a very interesting market and did not provide much variety. Market capitalisation is approximately £4,500 million of which the multi-nationals account for roughly £3,300 million. Although it is one of the aims of the Dutch banks to nurse young expanding companies to a Stock Market quotation, new quotations happen comparatively rarely. The reasons for this are that a good company has little trouble in raising the long-term finance it requires, and in any case the Dutch taxation system is no incentive to entrepreneurs. In addition the Dutch international companies are always on the look-out for successful companies and buy them before a quotation is achieved.

Foreign equities, mainly American, are usually in the form of CDRs (Continental Depositary Receipts) thus avoiding the necessity to register individual shares with the company. A Dutch Certification Office buys a tranche of the equity of a foreign company, registers it in its own name and then issues subscribers certificates stating that they are supported by the underlying share. There have recently been attempts to stimulate this activity in order that Amsterdam should attract a larger proportion of the international and more particularly the European equity market. The 2 per cent tax on these issues has been abolished and the four banks which are most active on the international scene, AMRO, Algemene, Bank Mees & Hope, and Pierson, Heldring & Pierson, have formed a new depositary bank. The fact remains, however, that although CDRs are useful to the small investor for whom the costs of dealing abroad are sometimes prohibitive, many of the institutions are of sufficient size to deal directly on the principal national markets. It will therefore be interesting to see what success Amsterdam has in developing this particular segment of the market.

Foreign investors can buy equities on the Amsterdam market without restriction, but have to deal through the O-guilder market ('O' for *obligatie*, a bond) if they wish to purchase bonds. This regulation was introduced to stem the inflow of foreign money at times of international monetary crises. The O-guilder market can only be fed by the proceeds of sales of Dutch bonds by a non-resident and it is therefore a market for non-resident guilders. The premium is generally around 5 per cent. While on the subject of the Stock Exchange it should be mentioned that the standards of disclosure of information by companies are high. The Stock Exchange itself has assisted considerably in this process and maintains constant vigilance on the accounts published by public companies.

Conclusion

The financial institutions in Holland are considerably more developed than in other Community countries, but one could claim that by concentrating on a pure financial function they have overlooked their role as watchdog over the industrial and commercial scene, and have failed to maintain sufficient direct contact. Reference has been made to the similarities between the Dutch and British financial structures; it would be fair to say that there are also similarities in present economic problems. The rate of inflation in Holland is second only to that of Britain within Europe, and the Dutch have the same problem in defining the true role of organised labour within a modern democratic state. This has made industry less able to adapt to the more rapid pace of change while inflation has tended to upset well-established patterns of investment and savings.

Chapter Seven

The Belgian Financial System

It is usually assumed, when discussing the EEC, that many of its central institutions will be sited in Brussels. This city already houses the Commission and NATO and is the European headquarters of a large number of multi-national companies. Brussels is well placed geographically and communications are good, both within the city and with the outside world. However, if new financial institutions, for example a European Central Bank, were to be sited in Brussels, one might be tempted to ask whether the strength and diversity of the local financial system would enable it to be used by these institutions on a European level and so build Brussels into the financial centre of the Community. The answer must be an unhesitating No.

The main disadvantage of the Belgian financial system is that the capital market is small and is dominated by government institutions, while industry and commerce are ruled by a few holding companies and their subsidiary banks. This monolithic structure does not provide much variety and has resulted in little financial innovation during the last few years. What diversity there is within the system is made more obscure by the fact that standards of disclosure are very low in Belgium. Large companies dislike giving away anything more than the minimum of information and the picture is further clouded by the fact that Belgian financial and industrial groups have a mass of cross-holdings.

On the other hand, companies in Belgium are bound by comparatively few restrictions and the government goes out of its way to encourage foreign companies to come to Belgium either to set up a centre for their European operations or to make industrial investments in Belgium itself. Foreign exchange controls are few—even though a two-tier market, based on the French system, is in use—and corporate taxation still amongst the lowest in Europe. On a personal level, work permits are relatively easy to obtain and Belgium must be the only industrialised country in Europe to offer foreigners a tax incentive; subject to certain conditions, 30 per cent of a resident foreigner's income is tax free and more may be exempted if he spends the majority of his time outside the country.

As well as this, Belgium considers itself a country with, traditionally, an international outlook and little nationalism. This is no doubt due partly to its being a young country, having been founded in 1830 in the aftermath of Napoleon. But it is also due to the internal cultural split between the Walloon and Flemish factions: the French-speaking Walloons feel more allied to French customs and habits and the Flemish—who normally would much rather speak English than French—to the Dutch.

A further aspect of history which has greatly affected Belgium, especially from a business angle, has been the independence, in 1960, of its only colony, Zaïre, formerly Congo-Kinshasa. Great fortunes were made by Belgians out of this country, the largest and potentially richest in Africa, and no major Belgian company or group failed to make substantial profits from its interests there. In the space of a year the Congo suddenly became independent, leaving the companies no time to diversify, and soon after independence it was plunged into civil war which made further exploitation of the interests there impossible. The effect which this had on companies' profits and on business confidence in Belgium may be gauged from the Belgian share index which was at 92 on the 1st January of both 1960 and 1970, having recorded a high of 104 and a low of 73 during this period. Today most companies which were heavily invested in Zaïre have diversified their interests— often not into other foreign countries but back into the mother country, where they have profited from Belgium's exceptional growth since the formation of the Common Market.

Holding Companies

Holding companies, originally banks, have always dominated Belgian business: the largest, the Société Générale de Banque, was created in 1822, before the formation of the Belgian state. During the depression years of the early thirties the banks increased their hold on industry, buying up their customers' practically worthless shares. It was this that prompted the government to pass a law in 1935 which forced the banks to divide their industrial participations from their banking activities. The latter were hived off into subsidiary companies, the management of which had to be totally separate with no cross-directorships permitted. However these reforms made little effective change in the ownership of Belgian industry and since then this structure has remained substantially unaltered.

There are several reasons why it is difficult under present conditions to wrest control from the holding companies. Firstly, any major move which a company wishes to make can be blocked by a shareholder having 25 per cent of the share capital. Bearer shares, which comprise the vast majority, make it difficult to establish whether large shareholders exist and if so who they are, but in Belgium any surprise move which these shareholders might make is blunted somewhat by the necessity to deposit and register shares several days before meetings—enabling the controlling shareholders to muster their forces if they see the number of shares registered becoming substantial. Then there are the enormously complicated webs which have been built up around the holding companies, baffling all but the most devious minds about the ownership of some of the companies. And finally there is the fact that the major holding companies are so powerful and ubiquitous that all independent Belgian companies must consider the possible retaliation before entering into battle with one of them.

These facets, together with the natural apathy of shareholders, make it possible to control and manage companies with holdings of less than 20 per cent. In the recent negotiations between some of the major holding companies—to which we refer in a later paragraph—Brufina was regarded as the holding company of the Banque de Bruxelles with only 10 per cent. Thus the Société Générale, with a share capital of approximately £77 million, can control assets of an estimated £2½ billion and by means of its close ties with the major industrial families such as the Boels, Solvays and Janssens, extend its influence over half of Belgian industry. Its main interests today are in steel (Arbed Cockerill and Sidmar), non-ferrous metals and mining (Hoboken-Overpelt and Union Minière) and in finance where its chief interest is Société Générale de Banque. This is a very different picture from that of ten years ago when the Zaïre interests were contributing over half the group's income and textiles and coal formed another major portion. It also has an interest in another holding company, Sofina, which has a wide geographical spread of interests, mostly in American public utilities, but with other interests ranging from oil to finance in Italy. It was in fact the bid for Sofina by another holding company, Compagnie Lambert, which revealed the powerful defensive mechanisms of the Société Générale. Friendly shareholders were quickly gathered by the Générale and the Lambert bid failed, much to the dismay of many young Belgian managers who felt that better use could be made of funds than investing in American utilities.

Despite this failure, the Compagnie Lambert has pursued more aggressive policies than the other holding companies. It is more of a financial investment company than a holding company in that it is prepared to buy and sell companies, and having been founded in 1953 it is more recent than the others. Under the guidance of the young Baron Lambert it has expanded its international interests, particularly in the United States, and it has good international connections through its

Holding Companies

SOCIETE GENERALE DE BELGIQUE		% of Assets
Main interests in %		
BANKING		17·4
Societe Generale de Banque (20·4)	14·0	
(Deposits FrB 186,909m, profits FrB 952m)		
Banque Belge pour l'Etranger (25)		
Banque Belge Ltd		
HOLDING COMPANIES		13·1
Sofina (25)	7·7	
Financiere du Katanga (7·6)		
Congo pour le Commerce (CCCI) (21·5)		
Union Financiere et Industrielle Liegeoise (62·5)		
NON-FERROUS METALS AND MINERALS		29·7
Sibeka (52·5)	10·7	
Metallurgie Hoboken-Overpelt (15·3 directly, plus 43·7 indirectly)	6·6	
Union Minière (5·9 plus 11·9 indirectly)	6·1	
Companhia de Diamantes de Angola (11·5 plus 5·9 indirectly)	4·0	
STEEL		12·9
Cockerill (12·9)	4·3	
Arbed (14·8)	7·0	
Sidmar (2·3 plus 29 indirectly)		
ELECTRICITY		6·3
Traction et Electricite (23·2 plus 19·2 indirectly)	6·3	
REAL ESTATE AND CONSTRUCTION		6·7
Cimenteries CBR (23·8)	3·3	
MECHANICAL AND ELECTRICAL		4·2
ACEC (6·4)		
Brugeoise et Nivelles		
OTHER		9·7
		100·0

Control: Autonomous. Large shareholders believed to be Belgian Royal Family, the Vatican, Prince Amaury de Merode, Count Lippens, Solvay/Boel/Janssen families.

Source: The Economist.

BRUFINA *Main interests in* %	*% of* *Assets*
FINANCIAL AND HOLDING COMPANIES Banque de Bruxelles (10)	29
STEEL Thy Marcinelle (28) Cockerill (2) H.F. de la Chiers	24
UTILITIES Electrobel (7) EBES	20
OTHER	27
	100

Control of Brufina: Cofinindus 15·6%; Compagnie Lambert 15·6%; de Launoit family?

Source: The Economist.

COMPAGNIE LAMBERT POUR LA FINANCE ET *L'INDUSTRIE* *Main interests in* %	*% of* *Assets*

FINANCIAL AND HOLDING COMPANIES
Banque Lambert (100)
  (Deposits FrB 29,372m, net profit FrB 167m)
Berliner Handels-Gesellschaft-Frankfurter Bank (2·3)
Brufina (15·6)
Cofinindus (1·3)
Finanziaria Italiana de Investimenti (FIDI) (17·5)
  (a member of controlling syndicate of La Centrale)
	16·3

PUBLIC UTILITIES Electrogaz (8·9) Intercom (1·3) Interbrabent (2·9) Electrobel (1·8)	10·9
OIL Petrofina (2·7)	10·3
RETAILING, FOOD, AGRICULTURE Interbra (29·3)	8·8
REAL ESTATE AND BUILDING	26·7
OTHER Dewaay, Cortvriendt International (stockbrokers)	27·0
	100·0

Control: Lambert family; Rothschilds, small stake.

Source: The Economist.

close ties with the Rothschilds. Its chief interests in Belgium are in property development, oil and finance, with investments in other holding companies. It is the latter which have prompted its latest move which, if successful, will give Lambert control of a group approaching the size of, and at present growing quicker than the Générale. This move entails the Compagnie Lambert merging with three other holding companies: Cofinter, of which it owns 51 per cent; Brufina owns 10 per cent in the country's second largest bank, the Banque de Bruxelles; and Cofinindus, which controls Brufina, and is itself controlled by the de Launoit family. The reader who wishes to confuse himself further can refer to the tables which list the chief holding companies' major known interests.

The Banks

The three main commercial banks are the Société Générale de Banque, Banque de Bruxelles and Kredietbank. At the end of 1971, the first two had about 1,000 branches each while the Kredietbank had around 650. This compares with the seventy-odd of the Banque Lambert, the country's next largest bank. All banks are opening branches at a steady rate. The banks carry out the normal range of short-term credits and are active in the management and placing of bond issues. In spite of the fact that all orders under 10 million francs have to be placed through stockbrokers the equity market is effectively managed by the banks. As a result of the 1935 legislation the banks' activities are closely controlled by the Commission Bancaire, a small body whose members are appointed by the government. Matters relating to the management of the national economy and the money supply are regulated by the Central Bank, but it is the responsibility of the Commission Bancaire to control other questions of banking business, for example the establishment of new banks, mergers or takeovers and the composition of balance sheets. The only investments that banks can hold long-term are bank shares, government bonds and commercial credits.

Like other commercial banks in the EEC countries, Belgian banks have been faced in recent years by strong competition from the savings banks and agricultural co-operative banks. Some of the savings banks in Belgium are privately owned and others are affiliated to trade unions. In view of this increased competition there has been increasing speculation recently whether the Commission Bancaire will relax some of the restrictions on the activities of commercial banks. One likely result however is that the matter will be shelved until there is some general consensus within the EEC about common banking regulations.

Savings Patterns

Table 27 reveals the savings patterns of individuals; as will be seen, savings deposits are the most important, closely followed by security purchases and property investment. Contractual savings are relatively unimportant and most of the investment in securities is in fixed interest stocks as the Belgians are not great admirers of equities. Because exchange controls are few, a large amount of money circulates via Switzerland mainly for reasons of tax avoidance and evasion and greater security.

Table 27: Types of Savings by Individuals

	1967 Billion Francs	%
Savings Accounts	36·9	33·4
of which Banks	(19·7)	17·9
Savings Funds		
(including pension funds and life assurance)	11·5	10·8
Property Investment	27·9	25·3
Purchase of Securities	35·8	32·4
Adjustments	2·0	
Net Household Saving	110·1	

Source: Annuaire Statistique de la Belgique Tome 91—1971.

In Belgium, as in certain latin countries, there is a noticeably different set of moral rules affecting taxes and backhand payments. No doubt this has been encouraged by the country's close connections with its former African colony, but it is nonetheless surprising to find, in such a northern country, groups which run entirely undeclared companies to handle their blackmarket affairs.

New Issues

Funds raised on the new issues market have averaged 75 billion francs a year in the last few years (see table 28). The public sector—mostly the central and local authorities and the public credit institutions—is responsible for a large proportion of the total, although its share has dropped steadily from 80 per cent in 1966 to 69 per cent in 1970. In the private sector the tap issues are almost entirely those of banks (table 29)

Table 28: Statistics on Issues of Shares and Bonds

(Billions of Francs)

	1966	%	1967	%	1968	%	1969	%	1970	%
PUBLIC										
1. State	13·0		12·2		18·6		17·5		10·5	
2. Autonomous Funds and Social Security Funds	0·4		12·2		9·2		10·6		12·2	
3. Public Credit Institutions	7·6		12·5		16·7		10·9		21·6	
(of which tap issues)	(4·0)		(6·8)		(12·7)		(8·1)		(15·2)	
4. Local Authorities	11·9		12·8		15·5		16·3		19·5	
(of which tap issues)	(5·8)		(9·0)		(9·2)		(9·8)		(11·0)	
5. Public Enterprises	3·2		3·0		5·0		2·8		6·8	
TOTAL PUBLIC:	36·1	(80·5)	52·7	(78·5)	65·0	(74·5)	58·1	(74·0)	70·6	(69·0)
PRIVATE										
Shares:										
Belgian Companies	3·3		4·6		8·5		6·7		1·9	
Foreign Companies and Investment Trusts	0·5		0·2		0·9		2·1		11·2	
Bonds:										
Tap Issues	3·1		6·8		8·9		8·4		12·5	
Block Issues	1·7		2·8		4·1		3·3		1·3	
TOTAL PRIVATE	8·6		14·4		22·4		20·5		26·9	
TOTAL	44·7		67·1		87·4		78·6		97·5	
Of which, total tap issues	12·9	(28·8)	23·6	(35·0)	30·8	(35·2)	26·3	(33·4)	38·7	(39·0)

Sources: Adapted from—Bulletin of the National Bank of Belgium, May 1972, and Commission Bancaire—Annual Report 1970–71.

THE BELGIAN FINANCIAL SYSTEM

thus putting them firmly in the market for small savings, while the amount raised by block issues is extremely low; this is because many companies raise finance from the special credit institutions or from banks and because the holding companies are particularly well placed to switch money from cash-rich to cash-hungry companies.

Table 29: Tap Issues of Financial Intermediaries (Bonds and Certificates)

	1966	1968	1970
	(Millions of Francs)		
Banks	572	2,963	4,570
Savings Banks	2,663	4,582	6,542
Insurance Companies	25	21	10
Mortgage Banks and others	255	1,298	1,259
Finance Companies	—	—	100
TOTAL	3,115	8,864	12,481

Source: 1970 Report of the Commission Bancaire.

In the organisation of the block issues the banks place about 45 per cent of the bonds with institutions. The rest is distributed through their branch networks to individual customers and this marketing is well organised. The banks are allowed to hold the bonds themselves for up to two weeks, which gives them time to sell them to their institutional and individual customers.

Government Financial Institutions

The Caisse Générale d'Epargne et de Retraite (CGER) is a semi-public institution which gathers savings and itself lends for investment purposes. The greater part of its funds (80 per cent at the end of 1970) is collected from private individuals by means of small savings deposits. It grants loans to approved societies for the building of houses for the lower-income groups, gives mortgages and makes loans for agricultural purposes. At the end of 1969, 43 per cent of its investment was in housing, 15 per cent in government medium- and long-term debt and the remainder in agriculture and industry. The loans to industry and trade tend however to be short-term to balance the long-term housing and agricultural loans. Crédit Communal de Belgique specialises in the provision of finance for local authorities, particularly those which are not able to borrow directly from the capital market. The Société Nationale de Crédit à l'Industrie (SNCI) plays a central role in the provision of long-term finance to industry and its position has been of increasing importance in the last few years. Like the Crédit Communal it raises money by the issue of cash certificates and bonds, in roughly equal proportions, to individual and institutional investors, and these provide about two-thirds of its resources. The SNCI has fifteen to twenty branches in the main Belgian towns through which it taps the smaller saver. It does not however take any equity interests in companies; this is done by the SNI (Société Nationale d'Investissement) which was formed in the early sixties by the government together with some of the large banks. This organism has investments in some eighty companies in diverse sectors, concentrating, according to its policy, in new products and services especially where those coincide with development regions. Its net assets are worth about £30 million according to its balance sheet but it is only recently declaring profits on its operations.

In recent years there have been efforts to co-ordinate the activities of the various government institutions, including the CGER and Crédit Communal as well as the Caisse Nationale de Crédit Professionnel—which provides long-term finance for small businesses—and the Institut National de Crédit Agricole, which provides credits for agriculture. As an example of the increasing competition facing the commercial banks, the first two of these government institutions have instituted a communal credit card scheme which guarantees cheques of up to 10,000 francs and they are studying further areas of co-operation.

Table 30: Growth of Resources and Loans of SNCI

	1951	1956	1961	1966	1971
		(Billions of Francs)			
Resources	13	23	50	72	145
Loans	11	20	38	68	130

Source: Annual Report of SNCI, 1971.

Table 30 shows the extent to which both resources and loans of the SNCI have increased since 1952 and the fact that both have doubled since 1965. The Belgian government has used the SNCI as a vehicle through which to provide cheap long-term finance for certain purposes. These loans are subsidised by a considerable reduction in the interest rate charged. The various laws passed in Belgium in recent years covering the subsidising of interest payments gradaully increasing the scope of subsidies perhaps gives a background flavour to the operation of the financial system which has come increasingly under the influence of government.

The extent to which these acts of legislation have actually helped Belgian industry is debatable because, as one Belgian banker ruefully pointed out, a large number of American, British and German subsidiaries have taken advantage of the special concessions.

Insurance Companies

Insurance and life assurance companies are other suppliers of capital in Belgium but have never played a particularly active role in the capital market. One Belgian banker explained that the management of the funds of insurance companies had traditionally not been a priority. He added rather unkindly, 'The responsibility of looking after the money in an insurance company has often been delegated to the company secretary and he will perhaps spend five minutes looking through the portfolio before going home.'

Table 31: Investments of Belgian Life Assurance Companies (1970)

	Billions of Francs	%	Limitations %
Property	9·3	12	} max. 65
Mortgage Loans	22·6	29	
Other Loans	2·7	3	
Government, Semi-Government and Local Authority Bonds	21·6	28	min. 15
Foreign Securities	3·5	4	max. 20
Bonds in Belgian Companies	14·0	18	max. 50
Shares in Belgian Companies	5·0	6	max. 15
TOTAL	78·7		

Source: Bulletin of the National Bank of Belgium, May 1972.

Life assurance companies' investment powers are subject to various regulations. They must maintain at least 15 per cent in Belgian government securities or SNCI or Crédit Communal bonds and not more than 65 per cent in real estate and mortgage loans. As well as this they are restricted to 50 per cent in company bonds and 15 per cent in equities, with no more than 5 per cent to be held in any one security. Finally, not more than 20 per cent may be invested in foreign public securities. Table 31 shows that mortgage loans form the largest portion of life assurance company portfolios, that investment in corporate bonds is low, and that in equities is well below the maximum level permitted by law.

Stock Exchange

There is very little general interest in the Belgian Stock Exchange and it cannot be said that it is held in high regard. As was said earlier, its performance has been unexciting, being adversely affected by losses in the Congo. The exchange itself has been slow to adapt to changing conditions and markets have remained narrow and choice of investment restricted. Members of the exchange number 500 and their average age is estimated to be over sixty; of the 250 firms only about fifty are active. The running of the exchange has traditionally been in the hands of the elder members to the exclusion of a small number of aggressive firms which have turned their attention more to the international market and to corporate finance advice, particularly the buying and selling of companies within Belgium. Their strength lies in the fact that they are able to offer impartial advice to families wishing to sell their business, unlike the banks which are too closely associated with their parent holding companies.

The Stock Exchange itself is small. Total equity market capitalisation at the end of September 1971 was £2,700 million; there are 580 shares quoted but of these only about thirty are significant. In addition the market in Petrofina alone is estimated to provide 25 per cent of the turnover. The ordinary Belgian has little interest in Belgian equities and when he does invest, it is often in a utility company which is closer to a fixed interest security than an equity. The individual share markets are run by 'teneurs de marché' (brokers) who specialise in a particular stock, but do not take substantial positions. Banks are obliged to put all orders for less than 10 million francs through a broker; this has resulted in the banks dealing in stocks larger than 10 million francs whenever they can in order to avoid paying brokers' commissions.

The reasons for the weakness of equity are similar to other continental countries. There are few institutions and therefore little institutional support to the market; pension funds are usually reinvested within the company, life assurance companies are inactive and do not even invest as much in equities as they are permitted. Companies themselves are not interested in the equity market and there is therefore little incentive to provide adequate information. Although there have been efforts to stimulate the equity market and the Stock Exchange, there are no real signs that any major progress is being made. Performance figures of the Stock Exchange are given in table 32.

Table 32: Equity Market Turnover and Indices 1966–71

	Average Daily Turnover in Millions of Francs	Belgian and Zaire Shares (1963 = 100)	
		'Au Comptant'	'A terme'
1966	70	88	75
1967	80	84	75
1968	133	97	101
1969	147	106	120
1970	111	100	113
1971	166	109	117

Source: National Bank of Belgium Annual Report for 1971.

The measurement tools used by those who are interested in Belgian shares are for the most part antiquated. Yield is the all-important factor, but dividend cover to the Belgian is not whether the year's profits cover the dividend, but whether they, plus all the previous years' undistributed profits, meet the bill. For this reason about 80 per cent of total company profits are distributed. Companies' sizes are not judged by their earnings or net real assets, but more often than not by their paid-up capital.

The interests of the public on the Stock Exchange are defended by the Commission Bancaire. Thus, besides its roll as the watchdog of the banks, the Commission supervises public issues of shares and bonds and the information given in prospectuses; and terms of offer documents have to be approved by the Commission. In 1957 its powers were extended to cover unit trusts; new unit trusts require its authorisation and it may impose strict rules on the composition of the portfolios. The Commission is active in the protection of minority shareholders and frequently puts pressure on companies to disclose more information, but in the absence of legislation little progress has been made in this direction. It does not however have statutory powers with regard to takeovers or other share dealings, these being held by the Ministers of Finance and Economy.

Unit Trusts

Unit Trusts got off to a good start in the late 1950s but their growth and image were disastrously damaged by the equity market slump in the middle-sixties and they have yet to recover. Table 33 shows that their funds decreased nearly 25 per cent between 1960–66 and have since then only slowly begun to climb to their former level. Table 34 gives details of the split between fixed interest and equities and reveals the high proportion (64 per cent) of money invested outside Belgium. Much of this is invested in the Eurobond market and one bank explained that a recent fund invested solely in Eurobonds has been extremely

Table 33: Development of Belgian Unit Trusts for the Period 1960–70

	Net Inflow/Outflow	Funds under Management at end of Period
	(Millions of Francs)	
1961	+191	5·565
1962	−22	5·097
1963	+126	5·590
1964	−44	5·655
1965	−777	4·820
1966	−187	4·220
1968	+61	5·006
1969	+148	4·751
1970	+29	4·442

Source: Commission Bancaire: Annual Report 1970–71.

Table 34: Investments of Belgian Unit Trusts (as at 31 December 1970)

	Amounts (in Millions of Francs)	Percentage of Total
Valuation (including accumulated income)	4,625	100
Division of Portfolios:		
(a) Cash	410	8·9
(b) Securities (by type)		
—equities	2,552	55·2
—fixed interests	1,663	35·9
(c) Securities (by nationality)		
—Belgian	1,239	26·8
—Foreign	2,976	64·3

Source: Commission Bancaire: Annual Report 1970–71.

successful. At the end of 1970 there were only ten unit trusts run by five management companies belonging to the major banks.

Foreign Direct Investment

Belgium has welcomed foreign investment, particularly in areas where there are structural problems and new investment is urgently required. In order to take over Belgian companies the permission of the Ministry of Economics is needed, and they usually require some commitment that employment will be maintained, but generally their approval has been easily obtained. The recent case where a British insurance company was refused permission to take over one of its Belgian counterparts was, happily, an exception, and it is as well to remember that other British companies have already made major takeovers in this sector and become a dominating influence in it.

Another area which has seen British dominance in the past few years is property development. The cross-Channel onslaught was led by a major firm of estate agents about ten years ago, and it is now estimated that half the main business street, the Avenue des Arts, is either owned or being developed by British companies. Nor is their activity restricted to that area: the exclusive Avenue Louise is at present seeing many major developments, again led by British companies who are making the most of the least restrictive planning laws of any major European capital.

Then there is that important commodity, beer: all the major UK breweries have taken over companies in Belgium to take advantage of the population with the highest per capita consumption in the world. And it is not only the British who have made major investments in this and other sectors: the French and Germans, and of course the Americans, have all taken dominant positions in certain industries.

Conclusion

It is hard for an outsider to be enthusiastic about the structure of Belgian commerce and industry, dominated as it is by the holding companies. Looking objectively at the results which this structure has produced makes one question its efficacy: a large proportion of Belgian companies are run by management with a distinctly seedy air; although Solvay and Petrofina may be cited as shining examples, Belgium has produced no real world leaders such as have emerged in Holland, Switzerland and Sweden, and there is little possibility for entrepreneurial activity to enliven the scene. At the same time Belgian finance is held in the straitjacket of government institutions and the ubiquitous holding companies. It remains to be seen whether the influence of Baron Lambert and foreign competition will be able to rejuvenate Belgium's antiquated financial structure.

Chapter Eight

The Italian Financial System

Of all the financial systems in the Community the Italian system is the one that contrasts most with the United Kingdom. In fact one could say that the Italian system displays all the characteristics which are most likely to disturb someone with a traditional City approach: the economy is dominated by a few state-owned holding companies; most long-term finance is raised through government-controlled institutions; the equity market has performed abysmally over the last decade and balance sheets are not to be trusted. Such criticisms are shared by a number of Italian bankers and businessmen, but it would be unfair to present Italy as a totally uninteresting country from the point of view of investment and savings.

In defence of Italy it has to be said that it has been one of the 'miracle' growth countries since the war, and although it is facing severe political and economic problems at the moment it is not the only European country with such problems. Furthermore, due to its geography it suffers from structural problems although great efforts are being made to overcome them, particularly in the Mezzogiorno. Italy is also affected by the fact that loyalties are still regional rather than national. Finally, the partnership between the state and industry through the holding companies has often been considered as a good example of the efficient management of a country's resources.

Any consideration of the financial system in Italy must begin with a brief description of IRI, the holding company which dominates many sectors of Italian industry, but at the same time is closely concerned with the financial sector.

IRI

The Industrial Reconstruction Institute (IRI) was set up in 1933 to assist with the reorganisation of the banking system which had been hard hit by the depression. Its initial function was to take over from the banks their participations in industrial companies on a short-term basis and then to resell them when conditions were more stable. Although it succeeded in selling some of the shareholdings in the first few years, the original plan could not be carried out, due to the variety of shareholdings in different industries and the difficult political climate, and in 1937 its statutes were changed to make it a permanent institution which would engage in a wide range of activities following directives from the government.

IRI's industrial activities are organised through five main subsidiaries, each of which is allotted a certain sector. STET is responsible for the telephones, FINMARE for shipping, FINSIDER for steel, FINMECCANICA for engineering, and FINCANTIERI for shipbuilding. IRI also has other important shareholdings including near total control of the three banks of 'National Interest' (banche d'interesse nazionale), namely the Banca Commerciale Italiana, Credito Italiano and Banco di Roma, and other smaller banking institutions, as well as other organisations including Alitalia, the Autostrade construction and operating company and RAI, Radiotelevisione Italiana. IRI does not, however, always take majority participations.

The main board of IRI acts as a buffer between the government and the operating companies. Individual companies are therefore given a considerable amount of freedom, but the government is still very much concerned when matters of strategy are involved. The other two principal state holding companies are ENEL which runs the electricity industry, and ENI which is active in the oil industry.

The Banking System

The principal banks can be divided into two groups, the public law or charter banks (istituti di credito di diritto publico) and the banks of national interest (banche d'interesse nazionale); this latter title is only granted when banks operate in at least thirty of the regions. Although their origins were dissimilar, the differences have now largely disappeared and both groups are active in normal short-term banking operations.

There are six public law banks and half of these date from the sixteenth or seventeenth century. In contrast to the public image of unscrupulous bankers of that era, they were in fact founded to combat usury and their profits were applied for charitable purposes. The Istituto Bancario di San Paolo di Torino, for example, was set up in 1519 to help the poor who had let their household goods, their clothes, their beds and the objects most necessary to their livelihood fall into the hands of moneylenders, while the Monte dei Paschi di Siena was founded in 1624 mainly to help the middle classes to cultivate their fields without resorting to usurers. The other public charter banks are the Banco di Napoli, Banco di Sicilia, Banco Nazionale del Lavoro, which has over 40 per cent of the deposits of this group, and the Banco di Sardegna. The directors are appointed by the government and the bulk of their profit goes to public welfare and charities.

The three banks of national interest have somewhat different origins. Two of them, Banca Commerciale and Credito Italiano, were founded by German interests in the 1890s and their capital was augmented by infusions from France in the early part of this century. They developed as universal banks and their industrial shareholdings were taken over by IRI in the reorganisation of 1933. Banco di Roma was established by a group of Roman nobles with a capital of 6 million lire in 1880, 5 million of which was lost in its first few years of operation. Further funds were injected in 1899 and it was the first Italian bank to expand abroad. All three are now controlled by IRI which owns 95·4 per cent of Banca Commerciale Italiana, 81·4 per cent of Credito Italiano and 96 per cent of Banco di Roma.

The size of the four major banks in terms of deposits is given in table 35. Banca Nazionale del Lavoro is the biggest with deposits at the

Table 35: Five Largest Banks in Italy

	Deposits, 1970, in Billion Lire
Banca Nazionale del Lavoro	5,425
Banca Commerciale Italiana	4,957
Banco di Roma	4,144
Credito Italiano	4,081
Banco di Napoli	2,127

end of 1970 of 5,425 billion lire, but this straightforward comparison is somewhat misleading. Banca Nazionale del Lavoro owes this pre-eminent position to the fact that following a decree of Mussolini all government departments must place their money with this particular bank. The official position of the Banca Nazionale del Lavoro is further underlined by the fact that it operates special departments for long-term lending, as do some of the other public law banks. This power is in sharp contrast to the general banking law which forbids banks from lending for more than one year, although it is known that there are ways round it.

The rest of the banking community is made up of smaller commercial banks numbering about 150 with 2,300 branches, 200 people's co-operative banks with 1,690 branches and 90 savings banks and pledge offices with 2,900 branches. These figures compare with the combined total of around 800 branches for the three banks of national interest. The savings banks and co-operative banks are principally concerned with providing a local service for the saver and the small businessman, and are able to complement their short-term activities with mortgage lending.

It is difficult to assess the competition in the banking world in Italy, but there is certainly rivalry between the major banks. Thus, during one credit squeeze rates of interest on current accounts, normally 0·5 per cent, jumped to 6 per cent. The situation is however now closely regulated by the Bank of Italy and rates of interest are set jointly. On a wider scale the Bank of Italy controls the opening of new branches and only grants permission after carefully considering the requirements of a particular locality.

Household Savings Habits

Table 36 gives details of households' financial saving, and it illustrates clearly some of the weaknesses and problems of the Italian financial system. Italy is a classic case of liquidity preference—that is the choice of the saver to keep his savings in cash rather than entrusting them to longer forms of saving—and savings accounts with banks and post offices, together with notes and coins, amount to about 50 per cent of the total. Other problems are easily identifiable. Firstly the proportion of investment in shares has been extremely low in recent years, and the total has declined from nearly 15 per cent in 1965 to 9·5 per cent in 1970. Secondly, foreign assets have increased sharply in recent years, largely illegally via suitcases full of bank-notes. It always was the prerogative of the Italian aristocracy to stack away part of their wealth in Switzerland, but the activity has now spread to the middle classes in a big way and it is not a hopeful sign of people's confidence in their country's future. The damage is, however, not as bad as it might seem because much of the money is collected by branches of Italian banks in Switzerland and shipped back to Italy. It is particularly interesting to note the sum of foreign assets (26 per cent) in 1969, a year of political instability, and the sharp rise in bank deposits and reduction in fixed-interest securities in 1970, which was a period of uncertainty.

Table 36: Analysis of Households' Financial Saving

	Amounts at end of	
Items (Billions of Lire)	1965	1970
Notes and coin	3,118	5,107
Bank deposits	10,117	21,596
Postal deposits	3,293	4,706
Other deposits and savings certificates	686	1,604
Fixed-interest securities	5,609	11,085
Shares and equity participations	4,839	5,851
Actuarial reserves	2,863	5,246
Foreign assets	2,397	6,676
TOTAL	32,922	61,871
Percentage breakdown		
Notes and coin	9·5	8·2
Bank deposits	30·7	34·9
Postal deposits	10·0	7·6
Other deposits and savings certificates	2·1	2·6
Fixed-interest securities	17·0	17·9
Shares and equity participations	14·7	9·5
Actuarial reserves	8·7	8·5
Foreign assets	7·3	10·8
TOTAL	100·0	100·0

Source: Bank of Italy Report.

Financial Intermediaries

In order to bridge the gap between the liquidity preference of the savers and the need for medium- and long-term finance for investments the government has created over the years a number of specialist credit institutions. By far the largest is IMI (Istituto Mobiliare Italiano), the shares of which are held by banks, savings banks, social security and insurance institutions. It is empowered to grant loans of up to twenty years, take equity participations in Italian companies and to carry out a wide range of other special activities, such as the administration of funds granted by the US Export-Import bank to finance trade between Italy and the United States, and the buying of Italian companies which are in financial difficulties. Two new subsidiaries for this activity were formed in the last two years, one of which is known as GEPI.

Specialist medium-term lending institutions are the Mediobanca (owned in equal proportions by the three banks of national interest), Efibanca and Centrobanca. Their lending is financed by savings of between one and five years and by issuing bonds; Mediobanca operates through the branch network of its owners and Centrobanca through the network of people's co-operative banks. There are a number of other special financial institutions some of which make loans available for depressed regions (ISVEIMER), or for particular industries or small companies. In addition some of the charter banks have departments for specialist long-term lending; this is particularly so in the case of Banco Nazionale del Lavoro which has, among others, sections covering long-term credit to the cinema, hotel, tourist, and other industries.

Tables 37 and 38 give details of the lending done by special credit institutions including agricultural and mortgage banks in 1970. Three-quarters went to the private sector, with half going to medium- and

Table 37: Lendings by Special Credit Institutions by Categories of Customers in 1970

Categories of Customers	Loans made during 1971 (Billions of Lire)	% Breakdown
Public Sector	411·3	23·5
Local Authorities	82·6	4·7
Autonomous government Agencies	62·0	3·6
Other Public Bodies	9·5	0·5
Public Enterprises	257·2	14·7
with government participation	213·6	12·2
Other	43·6	2·5
Private Sector	1,337·3	76·5
Main Companies	450·2	25·8
Other Enterprises	887·1	50·7
of which: households	300·0	17·2
TOTAL	1,748·6	100·0

Source: Bank of Italy Report.

Table 38: Lendings by Special Credit Institutions by Types of Loan in 1970

Type of Loan	Provided	Repaid	Net Increase
		(Billions of Lire)	
Domestic	3,364	1,577	1,787
Medium- and long-term	3,105	1,340	1,765
Industry and public works	1,973	947	1,025
Real estate	1,028	342	687
Agricultural improvement	103	51	53
Short-term credit to agriculture	259	237	22
Foreign	213	59	154
Financial credits	177	56	121
Lendings to non-residents	36	3	33
TOTAL	3,578	1,636	1,942
On behalf of the Treasury	868	168	700
TOTAL	4,446	1,804	2,642

Source: Bank of Italy Report.

Table 39: Burden on the Government of Interest-reducing Subsidies

| Sector and Object | Financial Years (Billions of Lire) | | | |
| | 1950–59 | 1960–68 | 1969 | 1970 |
	Average			
Industry, Commerce and Artisans	0·8	49·2	153·2	230·8
medium- and small-sized industries	—	12·8	27·0	33·4
industrialisation of the South	0·2	17·3	43·0	135·7
export credits	0·3	4·8	19·4	22·4
natural disasters	—	5·1	40·8	7·0
other	0·3	9·2	23·0	32·3
Building	1·1	4·5	13·6	13·7
Agriculture	1·7	26·5	59·3	66·4
TOTAL	3·6	80·2	226·1	310·9

Source: Bank of Italy Report.

small-sized companies and small businesses. This is a clear indication of the importance of this source of finance for a large proportion of Italian industry. In fact, the volume of loans channelled through the special credit institutions increased from an annual average of 280 billion lire in the period 1951–58, representing 9 per cent of investment, to 1,770 billion lire or 22 per cent of investment in the period 1959–1970. In addition, interest rate subsidies are available for much of the borrowing and in 1969 and 1970 80 per cent and 90 per cent of the loans by industrial credit institutions were obtained at subsidised rates. The cost to the government of these subsidies, particularly for the development of the Mezzogiorno, has increased enormously in recent years (see table 39). The degree to which these subsidies isolate the medium-sized and small enterprises from the conditions of the financial market can be surmised from the following extract of the Bank of Italy's 1970 Report.

'[The medium-sized and small enterprises] seemed to be most affected by the increase in interest rates; as subsidised credit has come to be their normal channel for the supply of funds, they show less flexibility in adapting their borrowing policy to market rates and therefore find themselves handicapped in making capital investment decisions during periods when the rise in those interest rates reduces the amount of subsidised finance which can be mobilised with funds in the budget.'

New Issues

By far the most important issuers of fixed-interest stocks are the government and special institutions, which accounted for 89 per cent of net issues in 1971 (table 40). Table 41 clearly demonstrates the severe shortage of equity finance in Italy, due primarily to high liquidity preference and general mistrust of equity participation on the part of savers. In fact equities outstanding only increased from 9,000 billion lire in 1966 to 11,800 billion lire in 1971, while fixed-interest securities increased from 15,900 billion lire to 34,000 billion lire in the same period. Pension Funds and Life Assurance, so important in Britain, are virtually non-existent. As a result an increasing proportion of finance is having to be met by government institutions.

The new issues market is controlled by an inter-ministerial committee, which in practice follows the advice of the Bank of Italy. This committee decides on timing, rates and conditions, and the banks are left with the rest of the organisation.

Table 40: Net Issues of Fixed Interest Securities

Issuers	1962/63 %	1964/65 %	1966/69 %	1970 %	1971 %
Treasury	—	26	47	42	45
ENEL, ENI, IRI	18	33	16	3	11
Special Institutions	69	40	37	57	44
Private Enterprises	11	1	−1	−2	−1
International Institutions	2	—	1	—	1
	100	100	100	100	100
Annual averages (Billions of lire)	1,088	1,713	2,900	2,610	5,040
Percentage of the total issues of securities (fixed interest and shares)	66	78	85	72	84

Source: Bank of Italy Report.

The Stock Market

From what has been said so far it should be clear that the stock market does not play a prominent part on the Italian financial scene—unless it happens to be the centre of some scandal! Italian bankers point out that the number of quoted companies today (144) is the same as it was in 1950, while the number of private companies has doubled. Moreover the industries represented tend to be old with low rates of expansion, such as textiles, and the new growth industries have not obtained quotations. In its 1970 Report the Bank of Italy dryly confirms this. 'As listed companies, whose capital represents two-fifths of the total capital of Italian companies, contributed only one-fifth of the equity issues during the past two years, it may be assumed that quotation on the official market, although in theory it makes the shares easier to realise, did not represent an advantage for the raising of risk capital during the most recent period.'

In terms of size the total market capitalisation of the Italian market was £4,000 million as at 30 September 1971. Its bad performance since 1962 is widely known. The index experienced a rapid rise between 1958 and 1962, fell from 1962 to 1966 and has slowly declined since, but the long-term trend has nonetheless still been upwards if 1953 for example

Table 41: Net Issues of Securities Showing Issuers and Investors

1971	Gov't & Gov't guaranteed	Local Authorities	Special Institutions	Public Enterprises	Private Enterprises	International Instits.	Total Fixed Interest	Shares	TOTAL
				(Billions of Lire)					
Companies, private and foreign investors	58·2	14·2	1,460·0	164·1	−32·2	17·9	1,682·2	966·0	2,648·2
Financial Intermediaries	2,175·7	12·4	769·1	397·7	4·8	17·9	3,358·0	6·1	3,364·1
Bank of Italy and Italian Exchange Office	731·9	—	5·5	185·3	−0·3	−0·6	921·8	3·3	925·1
Banks	1,388·1	14·9	702·8	214·9	−4·4	−10·2	2,326·5	2·3	2,328·8
Pledge Banks	−17·5	—	−12·2	−11·9	4·0	—	−37·6	—	−37·6
Special Credit Institutions	53·5	−2·5	20·1	3·0	−3·8	8·3	78·6	2·1	76·5
Provident Institutions	19·6	—	20·0	−3·7	−0·3	—	35·6	—	35·6
Insurance Companies	0·1	—	32·9	0·1	—	—	33·1	2·6	35·7
TOTALS	2,233·9	26·6	2,229·1	551·8	−37·0	35·8	5,040·2	972·1	6,012·3

Source: Bank of Italy Report for 1971.

is taken as the base year. The reasons for the present weakness of the equity market are not hard to find. Apart from the obvious reasons of the lack of institutional support, many individuals burnt their fingers in the period after 1962, and are in any case discouraged from holding shares as they have to be registered, thus making evasion more difficult. As elsewhere on the Continent standards of disclosure are low and companies have little interest in establishing a good stock exchange image since they can raise cheap money from government institutions.

Insurance companies and pension funds are not very active in the capital market. Most insurance company funds are invested in property while few companies run their own pension funds. One banker commented that the Italian government was far too sensible to let the management of pension funds rest outside its control.

Company Finance

Comments and comparisons about the financing of industry are tenuous as the statistics about debt levels are doubtful. The situation in Italy is even more difficult given the unreliability of published balance sheets and the further complication of different accounting practices. For example, in the official figures depreciation charges are added to the liabilities side of a balance sheet rather than being deducted from the assets and this obviously affects any ratios calculated from them. However, there is a general consensus that the indebtedness of many Italian companies is high with debt ratios often reaching 70 or 80 per cent.

Conclusion

One could sum up Italy to any British businessman wishing to operate there by stating that the risk–reward ratio is high. As a result of economic and political conditions in the past few years a large number of businesses are for sale. A foreign investor, unless from the United States or Germany, which have already made substantial investments, is welcome and could easily gain access to cheap money from the government. On the other hand of course Italy does not provide a particularly easy environment in which to operate and, to use a modern euphemism, its culture and business ethics are considerably different from our own.

Turning to the financial system itself, there is much that is wrong. Despite the plethora of special financial institutions it is sometimes difficult for good companies to obtain finance because of the bureaucracy and the need for the right contacts. There is a grave shortage of equity finance and a lack of variety of savings mechanisms firstly to attract savers and secondly to provide wider sources of finance for investment. These problems are recognised by the financial community and the authorities, but while the will to change exists, the means are lacking. Legislation in the present climate in Italy is an extremely slow process and there are other more pressing problems to be faced first. But although Italy could well benefit from the attentions of foreign financial institutions, it is unlikely that they will be given the opportunity, and Italy will have to find her own solutions.

Chapter Nine

Continental Financial Markets and the City

Continental financial markets, although by no means identical, nonetheless have a number of similar characteristics when viewed in comparison with the City of London. Overriding all else is the striking difference between the market orientation of the City and the state or bank orientation of the Continent with the possible exception of Holland. Whereas in Britain it is the free markets of the City which control much of the flow of savings to investment, on the Continent either a few banks or government institutions dominate the markets, leaving only a relatively small area for the interplay of market forces. These differences can be explained historically by the fact that those nations such as Britain and Holland which have for so long depended on international trade for their livelihood have developed a certain market trading mentality, pervading not merely the financial sector but many other facets of national life. Those nations, on the other hand, which have been more self-sufficient and inward-looking have been less exposed to such forces and have therefore failed to develop the same market approach. Whatever the reasons, this difference is reflected not merely in the structure of the various markets but also in the attitudes of those who work within them.

The volumes of funds flowing to continental markets from savers differ from country to country but are on average higher than in Britain. An indication of the orders of magnitude involved can be seen from ratios of gross national savings to GNP which are approximately:

Germany, Holland	27%
France	25%
Belgium, Italy	22%
United Kingdom	17%

As one continental banker put it, 'the UK has a good market but no capital; the continentals plenty of capital but no markets'.

There seem to be two closely linked practical reasons for the lack of markets in Europe. The first is that savers are traditionally loath to commit their savings to long-term investments, and the second is that institutions in the markets are not sufficiently developed to offer an attractive range of long-term investment possibilities to savers. Thus it is the composition rather than the volume of funds which is Europe's chief problem. Savers in most continental countries prefer to hold cash or short-term assets and the framework of financial institutions has been adapted to collect savings in this form and channel them to end users in the form of medium- and long-term loans. Indeed in France, Italy and Germany over half the financial assets held by householders are within the banking system. In France and Italy, either government institutions or government-controlled institutions dominate the transformation process and so can ensure that the requirements of national economic plans are fulfilled. In Germany it is the banks which dominate this process, leaving little room for any form of market interplay, with most forms of financial transaction—from money market operations to trust funds management and the effective controlling of equity markets—being carried out under one roof.

Thus most savings in Europe flow to financial institutions from which they are channelled directly to companies and rarely reach the open capital market; indeed when they do so it is often only to be transferred from one set of intermediaries to another. This process can be seen at work in France where the specialised institutions such as the public Crédit National issues bonds on the capital market which are bought by among others the Caisse des Dépôts. In Germany the volume of bank bonds issued on the capital market has been increasing; funds raised through these bond issues are distributed to industry in the form of long-term loans and 'Schuldscheindarlehen'.

The second main reason is the lack of development of financial institutions such as insurance companies, investment trusts and particularly pension funds. On the continent state pension funds tend to make less attractive individual company schemes, many of which are not funded, meeting their benefit payments out of contributions and have little in the way of reserves for investment. Further difficulties have been caused by the fact that the legal concept of a Trust does not exist in the 'Code Napoleon' and private company pension schemes often have their funds invested in the companies themselves. The unit and investment trust movements have been generally slower off the mark than they were in Britain and America. The IOS fiasco was a severe setback but the general view among continental bankers is that the worst is now over, and recently sales of investment fund shares in France and

Germany have been increasing. Life assurance companies have not played nearly such an important role with the public on the Continent as they have in Anglo-Saxon countries. Apart from tax differences, this may be partially due to the periods of violent inflation suffered in many European countries, but it must also have been affected by the fact that life assurance contracts in many countries were found to be worthless after the first and second world wars. The problem of making contractual saving schemes more attractive has beset most European governments over the past decade in their attempts to increase the flow of savings into long-term investment but to date they have met with only limited success.

This lack of institutional equity investors is one of the key differences between the British and continental financial markets. It has been estimated that British savers make approximately 50 per cent of their financial investments through the medium of insurance companies and pension funds. In Europe an average of only 10 per cent of savers' financial investments are made this way. Correspondingly in Britain a far lower proportion of funds is channelled to the banks in the form of liquid savings than on the Continent.

Despite this liquidity preference and the lack of institutional investors, European primary markets do work fairly successfully and indeed more private sector finance is raised in Germany and in France than Britain. The fixed-interest market is largely dominated by the public sector and is regulated in most countries to ensure that the nationalised industries and government projects receive preferential treatment. Institutional investment is closely regulated and much of the funds at their disposal are channelled into government bonds. In France, for example, the bond market is used to implement the government's economic policies and, even when the funds have been channelled into the required quotas of government bonds, there are further restrictions as to the amounts of equity that can be held. Much of the success of the primary bond markets in Europe is also due to an efficient bank distribution process by which the bonds are sold directly to their customers through their branches. In France the bonds of the SNCF are even sold at railway stations. There is however very little in the way of a secondary trading market for fixed-interest securities. This contrasts with the position in the UK where there is an enormous amount of trading in fixed-interest securities, although these are mostly in government stocks on the gilt-edged market, which owes its importance to Britain's disproportionately large national debt. (The London sterling money and gilt markets are discussed in the Appendix.)

On the Continent the public at large tend to view the equity market as the preserve of professional operators whom they view with distrust. It would be possible to increase the flow of funds to the market by altering the rules governing the activities of such institutional investors as exist, and this is now being contemplated in France, but it will take considerably longer to attract the savings of the average individual who, with the general redistribution of income in Europe, is now of key importance. The Segré Report recognised this basic problem and stated: 'The problems encountered today arise because not all countries have as yet created the conditions necessary to ensure that the traditional clientele of the share market is succeeded by new classes of savers and by institutional investors.' Perhaps the basic difficulty is that the banks have a virtual monopoly of customer contact and it is often not in their interests to promote the purchase of equities which will take away from their own more profitable forms of business for which they require deposits.

The plight of the equity markets in Europe contrasts with the position in the UK where institutional investors are both active and important. They have a flow of new funds to invest from contractual savings and this positive cash flow provides continual support to the equity market. A good market is ensured by the split in the functions of brokers and jobbers representing different interests, unlike the Continent where the majority of transactions are between banks and are matched on a mathematical basis by a single intermediary. Businessmen in Britain are also encouraged to use the equity market by death duty liabilities, close company legislation and the possibility of using 'paper' in the acquisition of other companies. There are less pressures on continental businessmen to turn to their equity markets and indeed there are often good reasons for not seeking quotations as this means providing outsiders with information—something continentals prefer to avoid. Equity issues are also generally more costly, particularly in view of the fact that the interest on fixed-interest finance can be set off against tax whereas dividends bear the full force of differing but discriminatory withholding taxes. In France and Germany the requirements for a quotation exclude all but the largest companies and in Holland the takeover tendencies of the giants have tended to frighten smaller companies. These factors go a long way to explaining why there are over 3,500 companies listed in the UK and only 830 in France, 550 in Germany, 144 in Italy, 400 in Holland and 580 in Belgium. Thus it is scarcely surprising that the market capitalisation of the London equity market (£47 billion) is larger than all those of the Six put together (£39 billion). However, a factor which the City gentlemen who point to the inactivity of continental markets tend to overlook is that the ratios of turnover to total capitalisation are much the same throughout Europe.

The difference between the market and non-market approach is not merely reflected in the different structures of British and continental markets but also in the attitudes of the people who work within them. Both businessmen and financiers on the Continent view finance as a means to an end—just another commodity required for the manufacture of a given product. In Britain on the other hand, the financial community tends to view money, or more accurately markets, as an end in themselves. Although this attitude undoubtedly makes for greater efficiency within the markets it is not altogether so certain that efficient markets are synonymous with efficient service. On the Continent the financial institutions are far more involved in industry itself and their emphasis is undoubtedly on the service-orientated process of channelling funds to end users, possibly at the expense of investors.

This difference of attitude and emphasis is a direct result of the source of decision-making power. In France and Italy this rests ultimately in the hands of the government bureaucrats who control the flow of funds to suit their economic plans; a major role of financial intermediaries is therefore to carry out the requirements of the national authorities. In Germany decision-making power, although not centred on the government, is again in the hands of a relatively few people in the all-powerful banks. The autocratic nature of continental financial decision-making contrasts very sharply with the British system, which is not overtly controlled but rather evolves from the free interplay of the various specialised institutions making up the market. This distinction goes some way to explaining why continental systems are set about by rules and legislation, whereas in Britain the forces of a free market obviate the need for red tape.

Most important consequences flow from this distinction between a free market and government or bank control. In Britain it is possible to influence decisions affecting the economy of the country from within the City, and the financial community therefore attracts a skilled and highly qualified work force. The freedom to operate within the confines of a market has also produced a number of creative financial engineers. New ideas and techniques are constantly being tried out, such as those that led to the creation of the inter-bank market. In recent years the restless asset-strippers and earnings-boosters have been so active that takeovers do not catch the public eye unless they are in the multi-million pound category. Indeed the buying and selling of companies on the British scale has never been seen on the Continent, being possible only with the existence of a thriving equity market. The very nature of the market also ensures that successes and failures are there for all to see and are given wide publicity by an inquisitive and highly qualified financial press. The disclosure of information is also of a high standard. Another asset of the City is the degree of mutual trust on the part of the operators which has led to the maxim 'my word is my bond'. As a result of these factors the City presents a certain glamour image to the outside world and while its performance has been impressive, it is well to remember that much of this success is directly attributable to the freedom from government interference and restrictive legislation which has enabled markets to thrive.

A French banker summed up the essential difference between the British and Continental systems when he said, 'In France you cannot do anything unless you have been given express permission; in England you can do everything unless you have been expressly told not to.' It is this factor more than any other which accounts for the lacklustre image of continental markets and the low regard with which they are held in certain countries. On the Continent, a career in industry or government is often more attractive to the intelligent young man than one in finance. In France there is little prestige attached to being a financier's underling outside the limited circle of the financial establishment; prestige goes with a high post in the Civil Service, and one of the most respected positions is that of the 'Inspecteur des Finances'—gentlemen responsible for seeing that the rules are kept. This has proved a most necessary function, for the very existence of red tape provides many with a lucrative livelihood in finding ways round it or merely breaking it. The end result is that those in authority do not trust the operators and the operators do not trust their fellow-operators; some southern Italian banks, for instance, may prefer to lend through London than direct to northern Italian banks.

There are of course fundamental political and social reasons why financial markets are strictly regulated and controlled on the Continent. Apart from certain countries' disenchantment with overt capitalism, there are major practical problems in transforming the vast volumes of short-term savings into long-term finance and the support of government institutions is crucial. Clearly it is difficult for governments to create or operate markets, and as the whole process of national economic planning is generally more centralised and controlled than in Britain, it is logical that the government should extend its intervention in the transformation process to the direction of capital flows.

These different backgrounds have ensured that the financial markets of Europe all have their own characteristics. Although there are considerable differences between the individual continental markets these are overshadowed by the profound differences between 'them' and 'us'. It is not the purpose of this book to judge the relative merits of the state, bank or market systems; indeed it is difficult to say by what criterion such a judgement could be made. But one observation seems in order. If it is generally accepted that the basic function of a financial market, whatever its nature, is to supply industry and the economy with finance to achieve desired levels of growth, then it is reasonable to compare relative performances. European growth rates and levels of investment have been very high during the past decade and do not seem to have suffered unduly from a lack of capital despite inefficient markets. Britain's growth rates and levels of investment, on the other hand, bear no comparison with those of Europe. There are many reasons for this state of affairs but it is unlikely that the City's often heard complaint of bad industrial management is the sole cause; some of the fault must lie at the City's door. There is always the inherent danger that too great a concentration on the market means that the City tends to lose sight of its raison d'être. To use the analogy of the racecourse—is it more important to have an efficient bookmaking system or good horses?

Chapter Ten
Future Trends

Britain's entry into the EEC will present those responsible for formulating common economic policies, and particularly common financial market policies, with some major headaches, for there is little disguising the fundamental difference between a free market system and dirigiste or bank-dominated systems. While it would be foolish to predict what continental financial markets will look like in say twenty years, what is certain is that closer economic integration will gradually force the various systems in use today to converge towards one common financial system and at the same time national rules and regulations affecting financial markets will gradually be integrated at Community level. We mentioned in Chapters I and II that the Commission has already investigated the problems of capital market harmonisation and is at present concentrating on further economic and monetary integration. From the history of developments to date in these fields we saw that the Community works on the basis of compromise and that national self-interest and pressure groups are the real deciding forces. Thus whatever the undoubted merits of freedom and flexibility, it is hardly likely that the continentals will stand idly by while European financial legislation is drawn up to suit the British, particularly when such legislation will almost certainly be harmful to their own interests. In any case it is difficult at the moment to see how financial regulations could be drawn up along British lines, as Britain's ignorance of continental financial markets is only matched by the Commission's ignorance of the British way of doing things.

To shed more gloomy light on the matter, the very flexibility of which the City is justly so proud may turn out to be a two-edged sword, for if it is really more flexible, the City will find it considerably easier to adapt to the inevitable compromises than will dirigiste systems, noted for their inflexibility. To make matters worse, the direct involvement of European governments in financial markets will mean that the City in putting its case will not merely be outnumbered but will also be negotiating not with its equivalents on the Continent but effectively with national governments out to defend their vital interests. Furthermore no single body has yet been established to decide on or to argue the British case. Thus while the City may hope to persuade the continentals that the British way of doing things is to be preferred and achieve a French sort of compromise, taking considerably more than it gives, its chances of success are not particularly high.

Indeed it can be argued that the free market system at present practised in Britain is in any case not suitable for adoption by the Community and indeed that Britain is herself moving away from such a system. The City is still regarded by many as the epitome of capitalism and in their eyes it is where the privileged rich become richer while the British economy stagnates. Despite its much vaunted ability to regulate itself, far too much money is made in the City through the sort of activities which should be considered beyond the pale by the Stock Exchange Council. Although Britain is in some ways—especially those connected with minorities and takeovers—considerably better regulated than most continental countries, there are opportunities to make what appear to many to be exorbitant profits through the exploitation of monopoly situations (stockbrokers' commissions being an obvious example), and through dealing with inside knowledge. This is not merely reprehensible in itself but attracts too great a proportion of Britain's all too scarce managerial ability to the City where it can be suggested its talents are not being exploited in the best interests of the country as a whole.

Although it would be totally unreasonable to attribute Britain's poor economic growth and low rates of investment solely to the difficulties of raising capital, reliance on market mechanisms as a means of raising finance can lead to distortions. Resource allocation under a market system depends not only on the market standing or rating of the borrower, but also on current market conditions. It can happen therefore that a particular company may find its ability to attract funds reduced for reasons beyond its control. The reverse is also true, for example in a bull stock market when companies can take advantage of high ratings to raise cash with no particular investment projects in mind, or alternatively do so in order artificially to improve certain financial criteria, such as earnings per share, which are held to be important by the market. A market system also suffers from the drawback that it can only think of an investment proposition in terms of risk–reward ratios and therefore cannot take into account social and technological factors. For example a market system will give preference to an investment project in a thriving company in the south-east rather than a similar investment in a company in a depressed area. In such cases the government has to step in and supply the funds which the market is unfitted to provide.

In a dirigiste system, however, social and technological factors can easily be brought into the decision-making process and this clearly has advantages when so many countries in Europe are faced with declining industries and depressed areas. Indeed, if ever the sort of Community regional and industrial policies outlined in Chapter I are implemented, the day of supranational dirigisme will have dawned. But a dirigiste system is by no means the ideal way to finance industry either. It has certain inherent disadvantages, principally in that it is bureaucratic, slow, unadventurous, inflexible and produces mountains of paperwork; it can be easily manipulated, and also offers ample scope for bribery and corruption.

Both systems therefore have their disadvantages, and although it is neither desirable nor likely that either one will give way completely, in some areas the dice at present seem more heavily loaded against the market concept than against dirigisme. The City which has thrived on its freedom from restrictions and regulations could find itself subject to restrictive community banking, insurance and investment legislation. Just as dirigisme is a way of life in certain continental countries, and their respective markets would be lost without rules and regulations and the necessity to have everything completed in quintuplicate, so British markets would be greatly handicapped by such restrictions. The nod and the wink of the Bank of England are a far cry from the instructions of the Banque de France and, more importantly, from the directives of the Commission.

Another aspect that may have considerable repercussions on the sort of system which finally evolves is best summed up in the old Persian proverb: 'Any fool can be honest but it takes real intelligence to be crooked.' Many continental financiers, talking freely of Swiss bank accounts and active personal tax avoidance, imply that it is the devious nature of their fellow continental operators which has necessitated such strict government control over financial operations. In England the capacity of the financial establishment to conform to a fairly honest code of conduct, together with its preference for self-regulation, has effectively forestalled the need for such close government supervision. However the whims of human nature and Gresham's law of morals would suggest that it is much easier to lower standards than to raise them. This may seem a somewhat frivolous generalisation but it may well prove to be of significance to the development of controlling legislation and thus to the non-development of free markets within Europe.

There have however been more practical indications of the way national barriers may be broken down and international standards set. In the case of banking, developments in Europe have been considerable over the past two decades and have resulted in powerful conglomerates all of which offer a wide range of financial services which had been traditionally handled by a range of specialised institutions interacting with each other in the various financial markets. There are now signs of the continental trend developing in Britain; the recent changes in banking legislation have at long last increased competition between the banks and will probably lead to the eclipse of merchant banks as independent entities. All the clearing banks now have merchant banking subsidiaries of one sort or another and merchant banks in turn have been trying to develop stronger domestic bases by diversifying into such fields as property, insurance broking and the like. British banking therefore seems to be moving towards the Continental pattern of department store banks, which must threaten the independent position of the specialised institutions. This in turn could have a detrimental effect on the good working of markets.

The difference between Continental and British bank involvement in industry is probably of even greater importance. We have seen how German banks and Belgian and Italian holding companies dominate industry. In France the Banques d'Affaires and Caisse des Dépôts have large interests and the clearing banks are increasing their industrial participations through their merchant banking subsidiaries. Like the American banks, these banks employ industrial experts and have the capacity to intervene in the management of companies in which they have participations.

In Britain the position is very different. Few banks are directly involved in industry and those other institutions, such as insurance companies, pension funds and unit trusts, which could influence large sections of industry through their extensive share portfolios have adopted an unfortunately negative attitude and have usually preferred to sell their holdings rather than interfere. British industry abounds with the somnolent giants of yesteryear, ineffectively managed by self-perpetuating cliques largely free from any form of harassment or encouragement by their absentee institutional shareholders other than through changes in share price. This stimulus in itself is of little interest to such companies except when they come to raise new money, and in any case in inflationary conditions share prices can usually be supported by asset revaluations and dividend payments. City gentlemen still tend to view themselves as a race apart from industrial managers with few being prepared to change their stiff collars for a pair of overalls. This view was reflected by a German banker who was convinced that the fundamental reason for Britain's poor industrial performance since the war has been the failure of the City to appreciate the relevance of the shop floor and he contrasted the position with that in Germany where the banks' close involvement in industry has had much to do with that country's economic record.

This criticism cannot be levelled at the newer generation of entrepreneurs running aggressive financial conglomerates. Whatever views one takes of their abilities at financial engineering, they have at least attempted to extract the maximum from the assets under their control. As they have been prepared to involve themselves substantially in industrial participations these 'predators', are much better prepared to exploit continental markets than their exclusively City-orientated competitors. However, it will be interesting to see how easily they will be able to establish themselves and flourish on the Continent where their style of stock exchange dealing is as yet unknown.

The City's concentration on markets rather than on the industry it is there to serve, coincides with a greater emphasis on equity rather than debt finance. Although it is very difficult to measure the relative gearing of Continental and British companies, for the reason that British companies disclose maximum earnings and assets in order to maintain a good stock exchange image whereas continental companies tend to do the opposite, it seems likely that Continental companies are more highly geared than their British counterparts (see statistics, p. 138). A substantial proportion of British savings is channelled into shares and the debt equity norms set by the financial establishment tend to favour equity and thus enable the stock market and its associated institutions to thrive. Although at first sight this may appear to be directly in the interests of British companies seeking finance, paradoxically this is not necessarily the case. The relative costs of equity finance in various countries depend on different tax, interest, inflation and earnings expectation rates and while these are difficult to predict, equity finance has historically been much more expensive than bond finance. Indeed some studies in Britain indicate that the cost for a company of bond finance may be 1 per cent in real terms after tax as against 10 per cent for equity.*

This would suggest, ceteris paribus, that the cost of capital to British companies is generally higher than to their continental counterparts. Whereas national gearing levels are of little significance in a closed economy, when barriers between countries are removed, less geared companies could be placed at a disadvantage, as cost of capital must be

* As an example consider a British company growing at 5 per cent in real terms

regarded as a cost like any other. The higher the gearing the greater the risk that in bad years earnings will suffer, although this should be more than compensated by the results of good years. However in a stock market environment such as Britain it is most important that a steady growth in earnings is maintained whereas in a bank-orientated country it is of less importance as the company's ability to raise funds is less dependent on stock market performance. Thus the proportion of debt in a British company's capital structure is determined by its needs to maintain a steady earnings growth, which is in turn dictated by Britain's equity market orientation, which not merely serves the interests of the financial establishment, but also protects investors against inflation. However, the picture is even more complex, as the raising of capital is rarely viewed in terms only of its cost and questions of risk are always present. It could be argued nonetheless that the process of standardisation with the greater availability of medium-term bank finance following recent changes in credit control will result in British companies having to increase levels of bond and bank finance in order to compete on an equal footing with their Continental competitors.

The question must also be looked at from the point of view of savers, who are notoriously conservative in their habits. Whereas a financial market can transform short-term funds into medium-term, it can rarely turn these into new equity money. Since on the Continent most savings

annually. It wants to raise £100 when inflation is running at 5 per cent. Then in one year

Cost of bond finance	Interest, say 10%	£10	
	less tax at 40%	4	
	interest cost in money terms	6	
less	depreciation of value of		
	loan due to inflation	5	
		£ 1	or 1% interest in real terms
Cost of equity finance	Dividend, say, 5%	£ 5	
	Due to company growth		
	capital is worth 5% more		
	in real terms	5	
		£10	or 10% in real terms

Capital gains tax has been ignored.

Naturally companies are not wound up after one year of operation. However, some value must be placed on the present worth of the company, whether measured in terms of a discounted dividend flow or of assets. In both cases the capital of the company can reasonably be said to be worth 5 per cent more in real terms, and this increase—inasmuch as it would not occur in the case of bond finance—must be considered a cost.

take the form of short-term deposits, this partly explains the emphasis on debt-finance and the reluctance of the deposit banks to enter into new equity participations, even though it would at first sight appear to be in their interest to do so. In Britain on the other hand a large proportion of the nation's savings is channelled into equities. This is not wholly the result of investor choice but is the outcome of the investment policies of the pension and insurance companies. Whether the habits of European savers will be changed when opportunities on a British scale are made available to them remains to be seen, but the process will inevitably be slow. In the meantime debt finance must remain the order of the day.

This is not to suggest that more active secondary equity markets will not develop on the Continent. In Britain the ease with which paper can be exchanged in takeovers has led to much concentration in British industry. The spate of public takeovers in recent years contrasts dramatically with the handful on the Continent and the result has been that of the sixty largest companies in the world which are not American twenty-five are British (see the statistics at the end of this chapter). However all this activity has not necessarily been for the good of British industry, as it is inevitable that operators can concentrate more on building empires based on paper profits rather than on the genuine industrial benefits which are obtained by commercial logic. It has however been very good for the City where substantial profits have been made.

The lack of secondary markets on the Continent has meant that the takeovers that have occurred have been mostly engineered outside the market. Wealthy families still control a large if declining share of continental industry and their companies are often unquoted as there has been little reason for them to seek quotations. There are however signs that continental companies are becoming more stock market conscious and the advantages of a high stock market price are gradually infiltrating their top managements; prestige, share incentive schemes, easier new issues and rights issues all glitter on the horizon. The ability to play the paper game appeals and certain continental companies already see the London equity market as a way of escaping the clutches of their dirigiste or bank-dominated systems. At the moment it is difficult to see how a quotation in London other than for investments in Britain can be much more than a public relations exercise, as the dollar premium and exchange control restrict the export of sterling. However, one possible advantage of a quotation is that it may convince British fund managers that continental companies are in fact comparable with their British counterparts and that it is not unreasonable for them to be valued on a similar basis.

The sophistication and skill of the City of London in running secondary markets has no match on the Continent and there is undoubtedly considerable potential for the development of such expertise. Family domination seems likely to decline thus freeing large blocks of inactively held shares and directly making for a freer environment. The mass of small and medium-sized unquoted companies could well be persuaded to seek quotations but if this is to be of any value to them, their attitudes towards book earnings and fixed assets will have to change fundamentally. At present both tend to be minimised, since by so doing management can substantially reduce the incidence of taxation and dividend payments and hence increase its cash flows, one of the main financial measures of corporate performance on the Continent. In Britain by contrast companies are encouraged to maximise earnings and assets by stock market considerations. Moreover taxation computations are unaffected by overdepreciation or other hidden provisions, which is a striking example of how apparently minor details of European tax legislation could have more far-reaching effects than is generally realised.

There are two other factors both connected with 'size' which will affect the long-term development of secondary equity markets. The first is the already visible trend towards bigger companies in Europe, which has not been supported by the emergence of new medium-sized companies to fill the gap. Indeed, certain studies have indicated that medium-sized companies will gradually give way to a mere two or three hundred multi-national corporations which will dominate world trade by the 1990s. Views differ as to the desirability of this prospect but if such developments do occur there is little doubt that they will reduce the opportunities open to investors and thus the significance of trading markets. At the same time financial institutions are attempting to reduce the number of small equity investors by persuading them to buy units and shares of investment funds. The institutions are increasing in size as are the blocks in which they are trading; these are now often larger than the stock markets can handle. Even in London the Issuing Houses have found it necessary to establish a computerised block marketing system called Ariel. Such developments can do little to enhance the long-term prospects of active secondary markets.

Thus in all the different financial markets there are many conflicting trends and it is difficult to make meaningful predictions. However the integration of the economies of the different countries is bound to have repercussions on the individual markets and it seems likely that even without the almost certain interference of the Commission, differences will gradually be ironed out. We have detected various signs that bank domination and even dirigisme will increase in Britain to the detriment of the free market; at the same time there are signs on the Continent that some of the advantages of free markets are being realised. What the eventual mix of these different systems will be is impossible to determine. In any event it will be considerably influenced by the rules and regulations agreed by the Community which, it should be noted, will not necessarily depend on the merits of any individual systems but on the outcome of political in-fighting.

Statistics

DEBT AND EQUITY ISSUES AND RATIOS: TAKEOVERS

	UK (*1970*)	Belgium (*1969*)	France	Germany (*1970*)	Italy (*1970*)	Netherlands (*1970*)
Debt Issues %	45·2	80·1		61·0	89	96
Equity Issues %	54·8	19·9		39·0	11	4
Long-term Debt–Equity Ratios %						
Debt	21·8	30·7	39	57	na	34·9
Equity	78·2	69·3	61	43	na	65·1
Successful Market Takeovers	249	14	15	0	0	na

EUROPEAN STOCK MARKET VALUES AND VOLUME
($m 1971 unless otherwise stated)

	UK	Belgium	France	Germany	Italy	Netherlands
GOVT/PUBLIC SECTOR BONDS:						
1. Market Value by Maturity						
0–10 years	34,300	15,833	na	6,535	11,650	1,805
10 years plus	32,000	6,442	na	23,166	35,000	5,414
2. Volume	85,505	1,032	2,647(a)	2,792(a)	606(a)	1,536
3. New Issues	8,560	3,430	2,902	7,384(b)	5,646	651
PRIVATE SECTOR BONDS:						
1. Market Value	10,384	2,898	na	19,420	1,450	(c)
2. Volume	2,183	15	(a)	(a)	(a)	(a)
3. New Issues	707	113	1,667	2,230	116	314
DOMESTIC EQUITIES:						
1. Market Value	130,541	7,449	24,314	37,577	11,354	11,749
2. Volume	17,800	865	4,510	5,208	1,697	2,749
3. New Issues	614	242	451	1,479	104	23
VALUE NEW SHARE ISSUES:						
1960–65	4,050	na	4,015	4,939	2,042	363
1966–71	10,179(e)	792(f)	5,630	5,882	1,098	160

	UK	Belgium	France	Germany	Italy	Nether-lands
NUMBER QUOTED COMPANIES						
1960	4,575	341(g)	977	628	180	356
1971	3,571	335	795	533	161	315
NUMBER NEW LISTINGS						
1960–65	600	11	114	5	—	na
1966–71	688	5	71	3	6	(j)
FOREIGN COMPANIES QUOTED						
Total	360	74	173	64	—	262
of which EEC	19	44	40	22	—	30

Notes: (a) Private sector included in public. (b) Includes $1,966m issues of special credit savings, mortgage institutes. (c) Includes private and semi-public sector. (d) Excluding investment companies but including Royal Dutch and Unilever. (e) 1967–71 only. (f) 1968–71. (g) 1970. (h) 1969. (j) 1969–71.

Sources: Belgium: Banque de Bruxelles; France: Banque Industrielle Mobilière et Privée; Germany: Deutsche Bank; Italy: Unione Adriatica di Sicurtà; Netherlands: Amro Bank; UK: P. N. Kemp-Gee & Company. March 1972.

POPULATION: GNP: SAVINGS
1970

Country	Population	GNP Current	GNP per Head	Personal Savings as % Disposable Incomes
	000s	$ billion	$	
Belgium	9,676	25·88	2,670	16
France	50,775	148·22	2,920	17
Germany	61,566	187·05	3,040	12·7
Italy	54,459	92·85	1,700	18
Netherlands	13,032	31·28	2,400	14·8
UK	55,812	119·85	2,150	7·8

Source: OECD: Main Economic Indicators 1972.

Conclusion

Faites vos Jeux

How well the City can perform in a United Europe will depend on the regulations constraining its operations and thus on how strongly it puts its case to the Commission and how tactfully it promotes it within the individual member countries. At the same time, if the City is to establish a truly pre-eminent position in Europe it must develop substantial continental business from a practically non-existent base. This it will only do if it sets out to discover how the continentals operate and adapts its market-based services to satisfy their needs. Inasmuch as any increase in the City's business will mean a reduction in their share of the financial cake, the continentals will naturally be on the defensive and although nobody we met on the Continent doubts the City's skill and expertise, many are curious to know how such talents can be applied to their own financial systems. Indeed it is by no means certain that the institutions of the one will suit the markets of the other.

Nonetheless the greatest contribution the City could make to Europe would be to convince continental savers of its ability to protect and serve their interests. This would not only benefit savers but would permit the City to take advantage of the major structural weaknesses of continental financial systems and considerably improve the supply of much-needed long-term funds to European industry. Thus it is perhaps unfortunate that initially the energies of the City are being concentrated more on the investment opportunities on the Continent. This will give rise to two major problems. The aggressive investment approach of the City has already led to a muted nationalist backlash. At the same time capital out-flows due to substantial investment abroad, if not matched by inflows of foreign savings or investment, of which there is as yet little sign, could put intolerable pressures on the British balance of payments and even call Britain's membership of the Community into question.

There is thus a formidable challenge facing the City both in establishing the right operating climate in Europe and in working within it to the mutual advantage of both Britain and the rest of the Community.

Nobody should underestimate the results of failure by the City to establish itself on the Continent as to a large extent its invisible earnings will be crucial to Britain's economic health. Indeed in the longer term Britain will only fulfil its potential in a United Europe if it capitalises on its traditional service-orientated expertise and in this the City's role will be of paramount importance. Although at first Britain may have to adopt a nationalistic approach, if the Community is to succeed, the City must use its skills, flexibility and inventiveness to help solve Europe's many intractable financial problems. Increasing demands for capital, the narrow choice for savers, the lack of institutional equity investors, the enormous need for transformation, the divided and inward-looking financial markets, the dangers of the Eurodollar market, and finally all the changes stemming from moves towards economic and monetary union and a common European currency—these are all European problems that will only be resolved if Europeans set parochialism aside and direct their various abilities to searching for European solutions.

Appendix

The London Sterling Money Markets

The diagram opposite shows, in simplified form, the relationships between the various kinds of financial institutions, and the markets which grow up as a result.

First we shall look at each market in turn and then at the way in which the Authorities contrive to control them all.

(1) THE INTERBANK MARKET

(i) *Constituent Membership*
The Interbank Market consists of all the banks in London, placing money unsecured on deposit with each other for varying lengths of time, largely through the intermediary of brokers for the sake of convenience.

(ii) *Function*
The banks deal in this market with a view to making a profit in the following ways:

to finance loans made to their customers at a higher rate, and for general working capital:

to utilise deposits taken from their commercial customers:

to take 'views' as to the future movement of interest rates, and more generally to borrow for short periods and lend for longer periods:

to balance out the fluctuations in their books caused by customers' transactions, so that even the shortest-term resources of the banks are earning their keep.

(iii) *Nature of the Business*
The vast majority of dealings, where the initial deposit is for a period longer than three months, are now done by means of the issue of a Certificate of Deposit. Only the authorised banks in London (not including the discount houses) may issue CDs, although not all banks do so. (Specific permission from the Bank of England is required before

CDs can be issued.) The banks that do issue CDs are known collectively as 'the primary market'. At the moment, the predominant issuers are the clearing banks, but that has not always been the case. In July 1972, of a total of £4,032 million CDs issued, 21 per cent were issued by the clearers, 10 per cent by accepting houses, 16 per cent by British overseas and Commonwealth banks, 16 per cent by American banks and 37 per cent by other banks in the UK: of the total of £4,032 million CDs issued £2,328 million were held by banks.

(iv) *The Nature of CDs*

The CD is a negotiable instrument which evidences the fact that a certain principal capital sum (minimum £50,000) has been deposited with the issuing bank at a certain rate ('the coupon'), and that the deposit will mature and be repaid by the bank together with interest at a certain future date, not less than three months from the date of issue. Interest is, however, paid annually for CDs which are for more than one year. CDs might therefore almost be regarded as very high denomination interest-bearing private bank notes.

The advantage to the depositor of having a CD rather than simply depositing his money is that he is able, if he so wishes, to sell the CD on, usually to another bank or to a discount house before the actual maturity of the deposit, thus gaining flexibility and a degree of liquidity which would not otherwise be available. In addition, for individuals and companies not classed as traders in CDs, the sale of a CD with accrued interest before its maturity counts for tax purposes as a capital gain (or loss), rather than the interest which has been accruing while the CD has been held being treated as income.

The advantage to the bank in issuing a CD was originally that it might get the deposit for a rather lower rate of interest. Today this is no longer the case but if the bank will not issue a CD, it may lose the chance of getting the deposit at all.

Those banks and discount houses who are prepared to buy CDs from the original depositor are known collectively as 'the secondary market'. Many banks operate in both the primary market, as issuers, and in the secondary market, as dealers. They may in turn resell a CD right up to the day before its maturity. When the holder wishes to sell his CD in the secondary market, the buyer will quote him a rate of discount (per cent per annum for the number of days remaining in the life of the CD) which is in fact the yield which the buyer will receive on the *principal sum plus interest* to be received at maturity. The actual formula is:

$$\text{Principal} \times \frac{36,500 + (\text{coupon} \times \text{tenor in days})}{36,500 + (\text{quoted rate} \times \text{days to maturity})}$$

It can be seen therefore that if the rate of discount quoted for the purchase of the remaining life of the CD is smaller than the rate at which it was bought, the holder will in effect make a capital gain if he sells before maturity, and vice versa, if the rate of discount is higher than the rate at which it was bought, he will make a capital loss. Note that the 'rate at which the CD was bought' means the coupon if the CD was bought direct from the issuer in the primary market, but it means the rate of discount at which it was purchased if the CD was bought in the secondary market. It is perhaps best to illustrate this with a simplified example:

XY Co. deposits £200,000 for one year with the bank at 10 per cent and the bank issues a CD.

Six months later XY Co. decide they need the funds earlier than they expected and decide to sell the CD in the secondary market. They are quoted a rate of discount of 5 per cent.

Following the formula on the preceding page, we can see that the proceeds which XY Co. will receive if it sells today amount to

$$£200,000 \times \frac{35,600 + (10 \times 365)}{36,500 + (5 \times 182)} = £214,648 \cdot 49$$

XY Co. will therefore receive £14,648·49 more than it originally deposited.

However, the accrued interest at 10 per cent which XY Co. would have earned on its £200,000 for the six months elapsed would only have amounted to £10,000 and it can be seen therefore that by selling the CD today at 5 per cent XY Co. makes a *true capital profit* of £4,648·49.

Likewise if the buying bank sells the CD on three months later at 6 per cent they will make a capital loss of £566·70 which is calculated as follows:

$$\text{Proceeds of Sale} = £200,000 \times \frac{36,500 + (10 \times 365)}{36,500 + (6 \times 91)} = £216,757 \cdot 54$$

The bank purchased the CD for £214,648·49 and they have therefore received £2,109·05 more than they paid. However, the interest which would have accrued at 5 per cent on the sum which they paid for the CD for three months would have amounted to £2,675·75. The difference is therefore a *capital loss* of £566·70.

A holder of a CD should therefore bear in mind that if rates move down while he holds the CD, the capital value of his CD in the interim increases; and likewise, if rates move up he makes a capital loss. Neither of these, however, affects his *running interest yield* which is the rate at which he acquired the CD.

If he decided not to sell the CD and runs it to maturity the movement of rates does not affect him at all, unless he is financing the CD with borrowed money. The interest cost of his finance may itself rise or fall in the meantime, thus affecting his running 'margin' (i.e. the difference

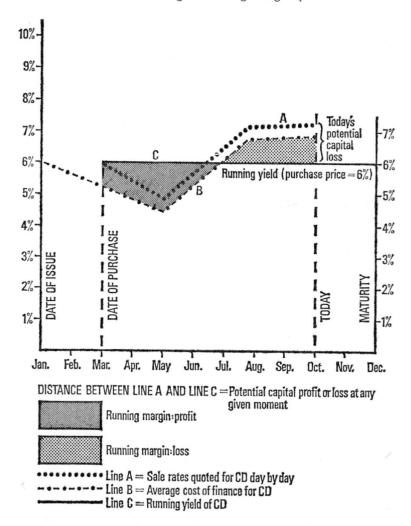

DISTANCE BETWEEN LINE A AND LINE C = Potential capital profit or loss at any given moment

Running margin: profit

Running margin: loss

•••••••••• Line A = Sale rates quoted for CD day by day
—•—•—•—•— Line B = Average cost of finance for CD
——————— Line C = Running yield of CD

between his running interest yield and the cost of his finance). In such a situation, especially where CDs are not often sold before maturity, the running 'margin' of the CD is more important than the potential capital profit or loss.

The diagram shows the relationship between capital profits (losses) and running profits (losses) on CDs. In this hypothetical case, a CD is bought at 6 per cent in the secondary market in March, two months after issue; it is run at a profit until mid-June when the average cost of financing the CD (line B) begins to exceed the running yield (line C). The shaded areas represent the running margin. With the benefit of hindsight one can see that it would have been best to sell the CD in June; even so, line A shows us that the rate of discount at which it could have been sold already incurred some capital loss, i.e. the distance between line A and line C for the remaining life of the CD.

The CD is, however, held till October (which is shown in the diagram as 'today') and we now have a situation where the CD has been run at a loss for the past three months. There is also still a potential capital loss should we decide to sell the CD, but as the CD approaches maturity, the size of the potential capital profit or loss diminishes, because it is expressed as a rate of discount for the future period left before maturity.

The decision which must be made today is whether or not to sell the CD. There is no way of being sure of the right answer which depends on many imponderables, principally the following:

1: Firstly and most important we must decide whether it is our view that rates will rise or fall in the period left to maturity of the CD. If we are in a position where rates have already risen against us, however, and there is a great deal of uncertainty as to what will happen in the future, various other factors come into play.

2: We may need to sell the CD in order to 'make room' in our position for other possible financial manœuvres which might be profitable. If so, there may be a good case for selling at a loss immediately.

3: If we sell the CD now, we may be able to repay any funds which we are borrowing at a particularly high rate and by doing so bring down the whole average cost of finance more than proportionately.

It can be seen that dealing in CDs is a fairly technical business; there are also further refinements, such as the 'Roll-Over CD'. In this case there is an agreement to put funds on deposit for, say, one year, but with a commitment on both sides that the deposit will be extended annually for say four further years. Generally the rate is fixed at the outset for the entire life of the roll-over, but in fact the market is very flexible in these matters. Individual 'legs' of the roll-over may be sold at any time, and, for example, the parties may agree that the length of the legs should vary, say the first two being six months and the rest one year. In addition, it is sometimes agreed that the rates involved should escalate through the life of the CD.

In spite of the complications of CDs which have been discussed in this digression, the original concept was to create a useful form of flexible investment for the bank's clients, and many companies still use them in a relatively simple and highly profitable way, as explained earlier, by selling them just before maturity.

(v) *Other Aspects of the Interbank Market*
(a) *Short Date Deals*
Where deals are for less than three months, it is not possible to issue CDs and therefore the business is transacted without certificates (or sometimes by using secondary CDs which now only have a shorter time left to run). A very large proportion of the market is in this very short end, particularly as banks all want to end each day with their books square.

(b) *Limits*
Almost all banks apply limits to the amount of deposits that can be put out with any one bank at one time, roughly in relation to the borrowing bank's capital and reserves. Special rules are applied to subsidiaries and branches of foreign banks.

(c) *Yields*
Yields in the Interbank Market vary over time, long-term money generally being more expensive. Rates vary little with the name of the borrower except for unauthorised and fringe banks.

(d) *Reserve Assets*
The reserve assets system is described in detail below on p. 151. For the present it suffices to note that Interbank deposits out do not qualify as reserve assets, but that the bank's net position (i.e. all deposits in less bank deposits out) count as eligible liabilities for the bank—i.e. the base to which the $12\frac{1}{2}$ per cent reserve asset requirement is applied.

2. THE DISCOUNT MARKET

The Discount Market differs from the Interbank Market in very many respects—its members, its function, its way of doing business and the way in which it is controlled. The most important distinction is, however, that Discount Market loans are nearly always made against *security*.

(i) *Membership*
The Discount Market consists of the members of the Discount Houses Association plus those houses recognised by the Bank of England as eligible money brokers and money traders. However, unlike the Interbank Market where member banks all do business with each other, in the Discount Market there is little reason for members to do

business with one another and instead the bulk of business is done with outsiders, namely all categories of banks in London.

(ii) *Function*
From the point of view of the authorities, the function of the Discount Market is to act as a buffer between them and the banks. This is explained in more detail later. The business of the Discount Houses is to trade in various kinds of securities—buying 'paper', holding it or selling it—and to finance its book with money borrowed from the banks. Almost always the paper bought is lodged with the lending banks as security for the loans taken, these loans being generally very short-term, if not actually at call. The object of the exercise from the point of view of the Discount Houses is to take advantage of the difference in interest rates which arises because of the difference in the duration of the loan taken and the 'paper' bought.

(iii) *The Uses of Funds*
The kinds of security in which members of the Discount Market trade and hold on their books is largely limited by the requirements of the Bank of England applicable to them under the reserve assets system. Under these regulations, members of the Discount Market must keep a proportion of not less than 50 per cent of the assets which they hold in the form of eligible short-dated public sector debt. This is defined as follows:
1. UK Treasury bills.
2. Northern Ireland Treasury bills.
3. Local authority bills.
4. Public sector bills guaranteed by HM Government.
5. Company tax reserve certificates.
6. British Government stocks and stocks of nationalised industries guaranteed by HM Government with not more than five years to final maturity.
7. Local authority negotiable bonds.
8. Local authority stocks with not more than five years to final maturity.

The remaining 50 per cent may be in any form of security, but again the choice is largely limited to the kinds of 'paper' which the lending banks are prepared to accept as security for their loans (although in fact Discount Houses do to some extent use money borrowed unsecured from non-banking financial institutions to finance commercial advances). In addition to the public sector debt money above, lending banks will take as security accepted bills of exchange, sterling and dollar certificates of deposit, preference shares and even equities (but only to a very limited extent). It is essential to understand the nature of these various kinds of assets so we will now proceed to examine the more esoteric of them one by one.

(a) *Treasury Bills* (count as eligible public sector debt)

The traditional function of the Discount Market is to provide the Government with short-term finance by taking up the weekly Treasury bill issue. In fact the Government uses the Treasury bill issue as a way of controlling short-term fluctuations in the country's money supply and the Discount Market acts as a buffer between the Government and the clearing banks.

Under the present system the Treasury bills are taken up by a competitive tender, where the banks as well as the Discount Market are invited to bid a rate of discount for bills payable by the Treasury three months from the date of issue. There is, however, a 'reserve bid' agreement, i.e. a rate at which members of the Discount Houses Association agree to take up any shortfall between the amount of bids received and the amount of bills on offer.

The clearing banks generally do not bid for Treasury bills in such a way as to swamp the tender, and in fact generally if they require Treasury bills they buy them from the Discount Houses instead, thus permitting a more orderly market.

Following the decision by the Bank of England to abolish bank rate as from 13 October 1972, the average rate tendered for Treasury bills forms the basis of the minimum rate at which the Bank of England will lend to the Discount Houses in last resort. In fact they take the average rate, add $\frac{1}{2}$ per cent, and round up to the nearest $\frac{1}{4}$ per cent, so that the rate is still effectively a 'penal' rate, i.e. higher than normal market rates.

(b) *British Government Securities*—'Gilts' (count as eligible public sector debt if less than five years to run to maturity)

The Discount Houses generally hold large positions in gilts but their holdings fluctuate very considerably. Until the advent of a reserve asset system these holdings were useful in that they could, if necessary, always be sold back to the Government broker. It is also the case that the bulk of the large profits made by the Discount Houses are generally from 'getting the gilt market right'. At the moment the Discount Houses find gilts less attractive than previously and the weak market in gilts is discussed in more detail below. The houses still find it necessary nonetheless to hold large amounts of gilts because of their public sector lending ratio requirement and the relatively attractive yields.

(c) *Local Authority Securities*—bills, negotiable bonds and stocks

The Local Authorities are very large borrowers and their obligations are in effect underwritten by the Public Works Loan Board (i.e. the

Government). The PWLB also effectively underwrites borrowings from statutory borrowers such as Water Boards.

Local Authorities issue various kinds of securities:

(i) bills which are short-term finance and count as eligible public sector debt.

(ii) unquoted but negotiable temporary receipts and mortgage deeds.

(iii) unquoted but negotiable bonds. These are issued for up to five years, and count as eligible public sector debt.

(iv) stocks quoted on the Stock Exchange and issued through specific houses. These count as public sector debt where redemption is less than five years away. It should be noted in passing that only Local Authority bills count as reserve assets for the banks.

(d) *Accepted Bills of Exchange* (do not count as eligible public sector debt)

The buying of Accepted Bills of Exchange was the traditional function of the Discount Market. Finance by means of Acceptance Credit is designed to bridge a gap, for example, between the purchase of raw materials and their eventual sale as finished products. An Acceptance Credit facility from a merchant bank today generally provides that the customer requiring finance should draw bills on the bank which accepts them (i.e. undertakes in any event to meet the bills at maturity) and arranges to sell them immediately to a discount house at a prevailing rate of discount, so that the customer is put in funds immediately.

If the bank is a member of the Accepting Houses Committee, the accepted bill qualifies as a fine bank bill and as such commands the finest rate of discount and is also eligible to some extent as a reserve asset (see below). Otherwise the bill is a trade bill the rate of discount for which is somewhat higher.

(e) *CDs*

These have already been explained. It is, however, worth noting here the role of the Discount Market with regard to CDs.

(i) The Discount Market buys a considerable quantity of CDs in the primary market (i.e. direct from issuing banks). These can be used as security for loans, and also provide a means of taking a view as to future interest rates.

(ii) The Discount Market buys and sells secondary CDs and in fact largely constitutes the secondary CD market.

(iii) The Discount Market deals in secondary US $ CDs to use as security for sterling loans thus providing a means of arbitrage between sterling and Eurodollar interest rates.

(iv) *Sources of Funds*

As was explained earlier the Discount Market finances with borrowed money the vast majority of the assets it buys. Some of this money is taken on deposit (i.e. unsecured) from insurance companies, hire purchase companies, other non-bank financial institutions and commercial sources, but the bulk is borrowed from banks against acceptable security. It is essential to understand clearly why banks should wish to lend money to Discount Houses.

The answer lies partly in historical convenience—the Discount Market, by taking very short-term money from the banks, provided the useful service of balancing out day to day fluctuations caused by customer account movements, but in fact before the advent of 'Competition and Credit Control' this function was already beginning to be usurped by the Interbank Market. The reserve assets system, however, has changed all this.

Digression: The Reserve Asset System

Before August 1971 banks in the United Kingdom were periodically subject to quantitative lending controlled by the Bank of England. That is to say, they were only allowed to increase their commercial lending to customers by a limited amount each year. The result of this was that it was scarcely worthwhile for banks to compete for deposits because it was difficult for them to find a profitable use for any additional funds that might be thus acquired. It also meant that many banks did not need to concern themselves in depth with the problems of liquidity since their lending pattern was strictly limited and there was a clear precedent to be followed.

Following the implementation of the recommendations in the Bank of England's paper 'Competition and Credit Control' the quantitative controls were abolished. The banks were now officially free to lend as much as they pleased, subject to the requirement that they maintain a ratio of $12\frac{1}{2}$ per cent of 'reserve assets' to 'eligible liabilities'.

The definition of 'eligible liabilities' includes:

1. Deposits in from customers.
2. The net total of dealings in from the Interbank Market less loans to the Interbank Market including CDs issued less CDs held.
3. Sixty per cent of the net total of items in the course of transmission less items in the course of collection.
4. The net total of liabilities less assets in foreign currencies.

The definition of 'Reserve Assets' is:

1. Balances at Bank of England (other than Special Deposits).

2. UK Treasury bills.
3. Northern Ireland Treasury bills.
4. Company tax reserve certificates.
5. Money at call: with members of the London Discount Market Association.
6. Money at call: with money traders.
7. Money at call: with eligible brokers.
8. British Government stocks (including stocks of nationalised industries guaranteed by HM Government) with one year or less to final maturity.
9. Fine Bank Bills eligible for rediscount at the Bank of England (not to exceed 2 per cent of total eligible liabilities).

One of the most important categories of reserve assets is loans at call to the Discount Houses, money brokers and eligible brokers. The yield on each kind of asset is different and their prices vary with supply and demand.

Reserve Asset Yields: (*example*)

UK Treasury bills	$5\frac{55}{64}\%$
Local Authority bills	$6\frac{5}{8}\%$ (when available)
Northern Ireland Treasury bills	Not available at present
Company Tax Reserve Certificates	
last issued January 1972 at	6%
Gilts—one year to maturity	$6\frac{3}{4}\%$
Money at call with the Discount Houses or money brokers—	
Day to day	$5\frac{3}{4}\%$
to	
Two months	$6\frac{1}{4}\%$

The table above sets out the prices at which reserve assets could be purchased on 16 August 1972 (that is to say, the rate which each asset would yield to the holder). It will be noted that money at call with the Discount Market earns approximately the same as most other kinds of reserve assets. However, because of the convenience explained earlier of lending in a very short-term to the Discount Market, together with the additional benefit of the loans counting as reserve assets, the banks actually compete with each other to place their spare resources with the Discount Houses who are consequently in a position largely to dictate the rate of interest they will pay.

Having established why the Discount Houses should be able to borrow such large sums of money from the banks, we must return to our examination of the Discount Market. Full implications of a reserve assets system are discussed in more detail below.

(v) *The Discount Market Assistance and Control by the Authorities*
(a) *The Dangerous Nature of the Business*
By far the greatest part of the money lent to the discount market is very short-term—either at call ('day-to-day'), overnight, or 'callable fixed money'. The discount houses therefore are borrowing short-term money to finance longer-term assets; this is only profitable so long as interest rates are stable or falling. Also, if the authorities decide to contract the money supply, the discount market may find itself short of funds as its usual sources dry up. This dangerous situation has always been recognised by the authorities, and in view of the usefulness of the discount market, special arrangements were made to ensure that severe fluctuations would not bring ruin on the market.

(b) *The Gilt Market*
Until the advent of the reserve asset system, the discount houses could always rely upon being able to sell their holdings of gilt-edged securities back to the government to raise immediate cash. The government broker 'stood behind the market'. This relief has now been largely abolished. The government broker will buy gilts with less than one year to maturity, and may at his discretion buy other stocks; for example if the authorities wish to expand the money supply. Otherwise, if a discount house needs to unload some of its gilts, it must do so in the ordinary way to a jobber in the market.

After the introduction of the new system, there was a long period in which interest rates dropped gently and as a result the gilt market was reasonably firm. In the summer of this year, 1972, however, it was felt that interest rates might begin to rise again. A lot of non-resident-owned money left the gilt market so as to get out of sterling which looked under pressure of devaluation. Prices in the gilt market fell, and the jobbers, expecting worse to come, sold gilts short, i.e. they sold stock they did not possess, hoping to buy it in even cheaper a few days later. Following the flotation of the pound, interest rates fell sharply. The reason for this was that with the devaluation risk removed, non-resident money felt safe in the gilt market where rates were high by international standards. As the money came in and prices rose, jobbers were caught short of stock and had to buy in at very high prices, suffering huge losses. Several jobbers left the market. Rates then began to rise again, and this move gathered momentum. The discount market, who were funding longer-term assets (with relatively small yields) with short-term finance at increasingly expensive rates, began to sell a proportion of their gilts. The result in a market unsupported by the authorities was a rather catastrophic fall in gilt prices.

Now the shortage of jobbers in the gilt market could in the long run have very serious consequences. So long as the Bank of England effectively underwrote the gilt market, the function of the discount houses and the gilt jobbers was largely intermediary. However, now that the market is out on its own, it will be necessary to have a fairly large number of active and substantial traders if the market is to avoid very sudden swings. The reason is that without a reasonably wide dispersion of views as to the future, the market is 'all one way' and this means a reduction in the marketability of government debt, which could only be compensated for by the yields on gilts rising even further. As a result, the government may find it more expensive and inflationary to raise finance through the gilt market than hitherto. This is a rather alarming thought when it is estimated that the government has a prospective borrowing-need of around £2,933 million for 1972–73 (*Financial Times*, 11 September 1972).

Undoubtedly something will eventually have to be done about the gilt market, but it is hard to see a move in the near future, largely because it would be such an admission of failure by the authorities.

(c) *Privilege Money, Direct and Indirect Help*

The discount houses have a right to raise money from various other sources in the case of need, namely the clearing banks and the Bank of England. 'Privilege money' is the term used for money which the discount houses have a right to borrow against security from the clearing banks. The rate varies, but may be as high as the penal rate which the houses would have to pay if they were borrowing from the Bank of England. It should be noted that the amounts of privilege money available are quite small.

'Direct Help' is money which the discount houses and eligible brokers may borrow from the Bank of England against security in the form of Treasury bills or Fine Bank bills. Money traders do not have quite the same access to the Bank of England as Discount Houses, but on a recent occasion assistance was given. The rate at which the Bank of England lends in the last resort used to be, of course, at bank rate. As explained earlier, however, this is now changed, and a much more flexible rate is used, based on the average of the weekly Treasury bill tender. In fact bank rate was already hardly used at all because it only applied where the Bank forced the Discount Houses to borrow for seven days— which happened perhaps three times in the last five years. The Bank is, however, prepared to lend overnight to the Discount Houses at market rates, and this it does quite often, although this activity is purposely rather unpublicised. It should be noted that the Bank of England has expressly retained the right to return to the bank rate system at any time.

3. THE IMPLICATIONS OF THE RESERVE ASSETS SYSTEM

In this section we will consider:
(a) the reasons for changing from direct lending controls;
(b) the way in which the reserve asset system was expected to work;
(c) the way in which it has worked to date, and
(d) suggestions as to the way that it is likely to work in the future.

(a) The Reasons for Abolishing Direct Lending Control

The chief complaint against the old system of direct controls was that since the discount market and the banks could at any time sell their gilt holdings to the government for cash, the government had no real control of the total money supply in the country. The Bank of England had tried to make up for this periodically by direct quantitative restrictions as to how much banks could lend to their customers, i.e. acting on the availability of credit and trying to control interest rates directly via the operations of the government broker. There is perhaps a basic flaw in trying to control capital investment by means of manipulating interest rates: namely that where new industrial investment is concerned, a project is unlikely to be undertaken at all if the possible small change of 2 or 3 per cent in the interest cost of finance will make all the difference between the venture being successful and profitable, rather than a loser. It is, however, a different matter if funds are simply not available.

Quantitative controls were at first quite effective, but the eventual result was the growth of the practice of inter-company lending; where one company had spare reserves, it found that it could earn more on these by lending direct to another company than by depositing the money with its bank, especially as the banks had an agreed cartel as to the rates they would pay on deposits. Moreover, they were not interested in increasing their deposits, because the restrictions would not allow them to lend out the funds so received. It was considered that the inter-company market was dangerous, because the companies were not real bankers, nor regulated as such and also because this new market largely annulled the effect of direct lending controls, so that again the money supplied was unregulated. There was also at this time a political feeling that the clearing banks were not sufficiently competitive and that they should publish their annual results in full. This in fact came shortly before the introduction of the new system, but the result was largely that the banks simply became more greedy, rather than more competitive.

(b) The Way in which the Reserve Asset System was supposed to work

The idea was that the reserve asset system should operate directly on the overall money supply. The availability of credit and interest rates would thus be only indirectly affected, and rates would find their own level in the market place. However, when the system was being put into effect, the Governor of the Bank of England was at pains to explain how he expected to be able to control indirectly the amount of bank lending. This was to be achieved partly by means of special deposits and partly by only helping the gilt market at discretion.

(i) *Special Deposits*

By calling for special deposits (i.e. blocked deposits at the Bank of England which *do not* qualify as reserve assets), the Bank would take liquidity out of the system, that is to say, the banks would either have to sell assets to raise money to pay their special deposits, or borrow more funds from outside the banking system. To attract these funds, clearly the banks would have to raise the rate they would pay on deposits; this would in turn force them to put up their lending rates in order to maintain their margins, thus theoretically deterring prospective lenders and controlling credit. To some extent special deposits would work on the availability as well as the price of credit, as the banks would be short of liquid lendable funds and would not find it easy to attract these quickly from outside the banking sector.

(ii) *Gilt Market*

Alternatively, the banks could sell assets to pay for their special deposits. These assets would probably be gilts, and without the government broker standing behind the gilt market, a fairly small initial fall in the capital values of gilts might escalate swiftly in a now essentially one-sided market. It should be remembered that as gilt prices fall, the yields rise and there is a tendency for other interest rates to come up in line with them.

(c) *The Way in which the System has worked to date*

When the reserve asset system came into operation, the number of unemployed in the UK was on its way up to 1 million, a figure which was politically unacceptable. It was therefore government policy to try to reflate the economy by massive government spending, increasing the money supply with the hope of this encouraging demand to pick up, and large-scale industrial investment to follow shortly behind. But if it can be said that interest cost factors are not generally vitally important when considering a possible capital investment, the likelihood of industrial unrest is often crucial, at least as to timing of the investment, in that it affects business confidence. Unfortunately, at this time the Industrial Relations Bill was becoming law and the climate could hardly have been worse for potential large capital investment schemes.

Nonetheless, the money supply was increased and bank lending controls were abolished. As would be expected, interest rates fell (and the discount market had a record year, financing long-term assets purchased at high yields under the old system with new cheap short-date money).

However, almost the only borrowing demand which appeared for the newly available funds was that of property developers and financial speculators, the latter encouraged by the political, rather than economic, decision in the budget to allow bank interest to be deducted from income and surtax. The vast bulk of credit went into the property market, where demand rose enormously. By its very nature, supply could not increase to meet this demand, so prices rose as the borrowed money chased whatever property appeared, and discussing house prices became a new national topic of conversation, rather like the weather. Worse still, because of the very slow nature of the transfer, developing and selling of real estate, the true size of the property inflation in the pipeline was not apparent for some time.

But as figures appeared for the actual increase in the money supply, people began to become alarmed at the size of the potential inflation. At this stage, say, June, the government could have called for special deposits and reduced the liquidity of the banks, thus drying up some of the new money supply, but this would have had the unwanted and indeed politically intolerable effect of cutting short any tender growth of incipient industrial investment. So the money supply was allowed to continue increasing; and as inflation rates increased, it became clear that people would no longer be satisfied with the low-level yields in the gilt and other fixed-interest markets, which had been caused by the massive monetary expansion. The result was that money began to leave the gilt market and this, coupled with the rather excessive revaluation of the pound under the Smithsonian Agreement, caused a run on sterling and the decision to float. Subsequently, the gilt market collapsed further and several jobbers left the market. Interest rates continued to rise. The money supply in the first nine months of 1972 rose by £3,380 million and the indications are that the increase this year will be of the order of 30 per cent. If one constructed a price index which included property values, the rate of inflation in this country this year would be truly alarming.

The point is that it was still politically impossible under the new system to apply the brake, because it is not selective. The only move made by the authorities in the autumn was a letter from the Governor of the Bank of England asking banks to channel their lending to industrial, rather than property or financial borrowers, but this received a rather cynical response from most banks.

(d) *How it will work in the Future*

One of the most significant and least expected factors of the reserve assets system has been the entry of the clearing banks themselves directly into the interbank market, and their massive CD dealings with the discount houses. In the old days, the clearing banks only operated in the inter-bank market through their subsidiaries. It will be remembered from the section on the interbank market that banks dealing with each other apply limits to the amounts they are prepared to lend to each other. These limits are set in rough relation to the size of the capital and reserves in the balance sheet of the bank in question. Since the clearing banks' subsidiaries had relatively small capital and reserves, the amounts in which the clearing banks could deal in the interbank market were somewhat limited. The clearing banks' balance sheets, however, are so much larger that these limitations hardly apply. The deals done by the clearing banks in the interbank market now are increasingly for fabulously large sums of money, borrowing and lending up to £150 million in a month; the effect of this is that rates in the interbank market can be moved very considerably by the clearers (although this is itself to some extent a limitation on their activities).*

When a clearing bank comes into the market to borrow such a sum there is obviously no immediate increase in the number of bank notes to meet this borrowing need and the funds must appear for the most part from elsewhere in the banking system. The result is a balanced escalation of the assets and liabilities of most of the banks in the interbank market, that is to say their 'books' are bigger. There is, however, no evidence to suggest that the deals are more frequent, only larger, so the average turnover per day in the interbank market increases, although the length of time for which deposits are held has not decreased. In classical economics it is accepted that the money supply (M) can be defined as the velocity of the circulation of money (V) times the average length of time for which money is held (T): $M = VT$. The clearing banks are thus effectively increasing the money supply in the country which is a prime cause of inflation. Furthermore, because the clearers' must now publish their full results, and growth is expected of them as it is of every other company, they must have a natural tendency to increase their interbank market figures still further.

Furthermore, the reserve asset system at present does not in any way control the growth of the business the clearing banks may do in the

---

* It is believed that on one day recently where a certain clearing bank was due to 'roll over' a very large sterling loan to a customer, the rate on which was tied to Interbank Rate, that clearing bank came into the Interbank Market and purposely bid up the Interbank Rates, so that its 'roll over' loan would be more profitable for the year.

interbank market. It will be remembered that banks must include only their net borrowings from the interbank market and net CD position as eligible liabilities. Taking all banks as a whole, therefore, $12\frac{1}{2}$ per cent of net liabilities and their net CD position must be held in the form of reserve assets, but since a large proportion of these reserve assets will be loans to the discount market, secured against the CDs which the banks themselves have issued, this limitation is largely nullified.

Turning to the massive CD dealings which the clearing banks do with the discount market, this causes considerable fluctuations in rates. The discount houses make prices on the basis of their current book which is in any event not really large enough to absorb the clearers' needs in full. Furthermore, when the clearers come in to issue CDs en masse the discount houses move the price fast against them because when taking in CDs the discount houses must balance these against purchases of government sector debt. Massive issuing of CDs by the clearers therefore tends to raise the price of gilts in particular (i.e. yields fall) and massive purchase of CDs by the clearers has the reverse effect.

The main problems that emerge from the present system are therefore:

1. That the clearers are able to influence the money supply at a time when the Bank of England is politically unable to call for special deposits.

2. The use of CDs as security by the discount market means that the discount market's relation to the clearing banks is becoming less attached to the industrial realities of bill finance and more of a card house built with CDs, which could all too easily fall down in the case of serious political or economic crisis.

3. There is a feeling that the authorities have to some extent abandoned control of the financial markets. The growth in CD business, which may not have been foreseen by the authorities, has now come to a point where it resembles more and more the issuing of private bank notes for the benefit of the interbank and discount markets rather than as a service to provide flexibility for industrial customers. The gilt market is equally unregulated, and has a built-in instability, which will eventually restrict the marketability of government debt, creating problems when the government requires longer-term finance. Its only alternative is increased taxation, which again is generally politically impossible.

4. Perhaps most dangerous of all is the likely increase of 30 per cent in the money supply in one year. Steps will have to be taken to avoid a truly vicious inflationary spiral, and sooner rather than later. It is true that the rates for the autumn months have shown a tendency for

the rate of increase in the money supply to decline, and this together with the price freeze of the government may head off the crisis. But it is the avowed intent of the Chancellor of the Exchequer to achieve 5 per cent per annum growth in the UK economy for two years at least, and it must be doubtful whether inflation and the militant nature of the unions will permit this, at least in real, rather than money terms.

5. UK industrial growth rates have, as is well known, been among the lowest in Europe for some years. Now, the increasingly important question as to whether economic growth is really desirable or not is an emotional and political subject which we cannot discuss here, but it is fair to say that a soundly prosperous money market must stand on the foundation of properly financed industrial expansion. If this continues to be absent for reasons such as industrial unrest, and general fears of inflation and lack of confidence, we will eventually have to return to selective lending control.

It is likely then that until industrial demand picks up or special deposits are called for, interest rates will have a built-in tendency to fall, because of the ever-buoyant money supply. The imposition of controls or the return of the government broker to the gilt market could, however, come sooner than might be expected and even the fear of this might have the result of raising rates very dramatically.

Index